THE IN(COMPLETE) ARC

A PATIENT'S PERSPECTIVE ON LIVING WITH SCHIZOPHRENIA AND THE GAPS IN INDIA'S MENTAL HEALTH SYSTEM

SAKSHI.K

Made with ♥ on the Notion Press Platform
www.notionpress.com

Contents

Contents

Preface

This book is written by the author from an objective lens. It is well researched and thoughtfully developed, though interspersed with the author's lived experiences, which should be construed as opinions disclosed in the author's notes. This book does not intend to be a sob story. It is written as the work of a survivor, researcher, and patient within the framework of the Indian Mental Healthcare Act, 2017.

The book aims to serve as a manual for people living with schizophrenia spectrum conditions, addressing common myths surrounding the ailment, certain biases, and prevailing medical practices. It should be viewed both from a researcher's lens and from the lens of lived, subjective experience.

Though Mental Health Awareness Day is observed every year and marathons are organised, stigma around serious mental illness persists. The person running next to you may carry one or more conditions within the mental health spectrum. Behind every smile, there may be an aching heart. It is extremely difficult for people with serious mental health conditions, often perceived as posing safety concerns to others, such as manic depression, bipolar disorder, and schizophrenia, to come forward and accept their condition. I camouflaged my condition for six years until it became unbearable to hide. On the pretext of supposed aggression, the rights of such individuals are often subverted in the name of care. From my observation, psychiatric care in many cases continues to lean toward restraint rather than open communication.

Other conditions within the spectrum, such as anxiety, ADHD, and certain compulsive disorders, where individuals are not presumed to be aggressive, appear to be better tolerated in the workplace and in society at large. This is a step in the right direction.

However, the pain behind manic depression, bipolar disorder, and schizophrenia is rarely discussed. Treatments are often driven by coercion and relentless medication and procedures. These can be physically strenuous, particularly for female bodies. In my opinion and observation, there is little distinction in treatment approaches between men, who may have greater physical strength and perceived aggression, and women, who are hormonally different. There are more men than women diagnosed with these conditions, and more male psychiatrists as well. As a result, female physiology, including my own, is often overlooked.

This does not mean that there is no middle ground, or that stress triggers cannot be managed, or that episodes cannot be moderated, if not avoided altogether. I have explored certain techniques in this book, based on my own experiments, which have shown some improvement in my overall health and stress management. I advise readers to seek medical guidance before adopting any such practices, as these are subjective and rooted in my cultural context.

That said, I do not believe schizophrenia is the worst thing that can happen to a person. It is still considered treatable, though perhaps not reversible, as it often leaves a lasting mark and the sting of stigma among those aware of one's condition. Monitoring one's thoughts and beginning with acceptance is important. However, this does not mean that human and fundamental rights should be violated. It also does not mean that consent should be violated, which I believe occurred in my own case.

As the book unfolds, I will periodically include opinions and anecdotes as author's notes. These should be considered subjective, though subjectivity itself is a fact. It is my lived reality.

This book contains details of my personal and subjective experience. Every individual has their own trajectory of healing and their own experience with care providers. Accordingly, my experience should not be construed as a blanket opinion, but as my personal account of mental health care in India.

This book is in no way a replacement for expert medical advice. Any information construed as advice should be cross-verified with a treating psychiatrist or a qualified medical professional.

Acknowledgements

This book is dedicated to fellow patients, wherever you may be. I hope it reaches you and offers some measure of solidarity and strength.

I am grateful to the patients I met abroad during my hospitalization. Our conversations, and at times our disagreements, broadened my understanding of the condition I live with. Witnessing others in acute episodic states gave me insight into my own reactions and vulnerabilities.

During my admission abroad, I was not subjected to invasive procedures without my consent. Some interventions were suggested by the medical team, but my stance was respected. As a result, my memory of not only the delusions but also of understanding, growth, and recovery remained intact.

I learned more from co-patients and nurses than from anyone else during that period.

I also believe that in many developed countries, patient rights and redressal mechanisms are far stricter and stronger than they are in India. I explore this aspect in greater detail in the book.

During my two hospitalizations in India, I experienced procedures that were carried out without my consent and which I experienced as coercive and invasive. These interventions led to permanent memory loss for the treatment duration and for a few days afterward. I remember being coerced into the hospital, but I do not remember the treatment itself, the treatment team, or even my walk outside the hospital at discharge. This disrupted my personal narrative. As a result, I have no recollection of meeting co-patients or anyone during that period.

Through this book, I want to raise a broader systemic issue within the Indian mental health care scenario: invasion of personal space, consent overrides, and adult rights being set aside. More importantly, after treatment ends, the memories of delusions and coercive admission remain intact, while the therapy itself does not.

Healing still seems distant.

Disclaimer

This book is based on both personal experience and research. It presents a patient-centric perspective on mental health rights in India.

This work is not intended to replace medical advice, diagnosis, or professional consultation.

The views expressed are the author's own and are shared to encourage diversity of perspective and informed discussion.

All personal accounts are anecdotal. Clinical details of psychotic episodes are intentionally omitted in order to preserve personal privacy and narrative boundaries.

This book reflects a patient's systemic perspective.

Dedication To Fellow Patients

To the heart that cried without remembrance;
To the body that shook, trembling with electric current;
To the uncalled sedation;
To the pseudo-emergency and showdown;

To the cranked neck that never fails to crack;
To the knees that cannot take the stairs;
To the headache that needs a painkiller;
To the weight that breaks the scale;
To the weak heart and high blood sugar;
To the sleepless nights of chronic insomnia;

To the system that simply denies;
To the power that is beyond, yet within my reach;
I miss my natural sleep and my natural body;
I do not seek a peaceful ending;
I seek redemption, someday.

Dedication To Fellow Patients

Life is...

A potluck of surprises;
An invitation to smile;
An opportunity to seize;

But...

One gets lost in the maze of competition;
One becomes jealous, insecure, and greedy;
One turns negative and angry at failure;

Then...

Opportunity strikes again, this time as an ailment;
When nothing but health becomes the epicenter;
When you wish to lift your fragmented body, yet feel too weak;
When your consent is overridden, and your rights are violated;

The misunderstood you then asks:

What did life make of me? Or did I make it so?

It is not the damage of a soloist; often it is colossal, disguised as rebukes and insults from the one you trusted most.

Life then becomes what you make of it, by prioritizing your rights and maintaining distance.

CHAPTER ONE

UNDERSTANDING THE DIAGNOSIS

What is Schizophrenia?

Schizophrenia is a mental health disorder often characterised by unusual patterns of behaviour, which may include changes in speech, posture, and movement. It is clinically understood through the presence of what are referred to as positive and negative symptoms.

Positive symptoms refer to the presence of certain experiences such as delusions, hallucinations (auditory or sensory), and movement-related disturbances such as catatonia. The term positive here implies the existence of external symptoms that are absent if the behaviour were normal. These are additional behavioural symptoms to look for. The psychiatrists look for the existence of these traits to diagnose.

Negative symptoms include symptoms such as lack of pleasure and focus, trouble with speech, and social withdrawal. The negative implies a deviation from certain behaviours that are considered normal in day-to-day life. The psychiatrists look for the absence of these traits to diagnose.

The presence of these symptoms is often associated with psychosis. Each occurrence of psychosis is commonly referred to as an episode, a term frequently used in clinical settings.

The causation of schizophrenia remains a subject of ongoing research. However, a widely accepted understanding links the manifestation of symptoms to imbalances in dopamine activity in the brain. As a result, most medications prescribed for schizophrenia, particularly antipsychotics, aim to regulate dopamine levels. While these medicines can be effective in controlling symptoms and aiding remission, they may also have significant side effects that impact the overall quality of life of individuals living with this condition.

Beyond the neurological impact, it is often the psychological aftermath of psychotic episodes that leaves patients feeling unsettled even after remission. Challenges may include experiences of rights violations, limited participation in treatment decisions, and the stigma associated with returning to everyday life after diagnosis. This is particularly common in Indian mental health care.

As noted by the World Health Organization and reflected in lived experiences, these issues can add layers of distress beyond the illness itself.

While clinical definitions of schizophrenia emphasise hallucinations and delusional beliefs, it is important for healthcare professionals and family members to recognise that, in the moment, these experiences feel internally real to the patient. One constructive way to address such thought patterns is through measured awareness-building and supportive talk therapy, where beliefs are approached with patience and compassion rather than confrontation. **Carefully presented external references, such as everyday news, media, or observable evidence from the outside world, can sometimes help re-anchor perception in shared reality.** Complex cases require thoughtful, individualised care, and lasting outcomes are more likely when treatment approaches prioritise understanding, consent, and dignity.

Gender profile and onset

Research suggests that the onset of schizophrenia commonly occurs during adolescence and early adulthood. It is observed that schizophrenia is slightly more common in men, with men also tending to have an earlier age of onset compared to women.

Is it genetic?

This can be genetic. The chances increase if a parent or sibling has this ailment, thereby raising susceptibility. However, genes are not the only factor, and environmental triggers play a significant role. Stress and major life setbacks are also considered contributing factors in the development of this ailment. Historically, genetic factors have been shown through studies to play a role in increasing susceptibility.

Difference between an episode, remission, and relapse

An episode refers to the active state of the ailment, during which symptoms are present and may include delusions, hallucinations, and changes in movement or behaviour. In some cases, the severity of an episode may require clinical intervention, including hospital-based care. Remission refers to the reduction or absence of these symptoms. Relapse refers to the re-emergence or worsening of symptoms after a period of remission.

CHAPTER TWO

THE TRIGGERS

Besides genetics, there are several environmental factors that are believed to be associated with the onset or exacerbation of schizophrenia, particularly during adolescence or adulthood. Early-life stressors, including unresolved childhood issues or trauma, have been linked to an increased vulnerability to various mental health conditions, including schizophrenia, though they are not considered standalone causes.

The author believes that the following factors may act as triggers or contributing influences that can aggravate mental health difficulties later in life, including but not limited to schizophrenia:

1. Childhood trauma, including verbal or physical abuse
2. Childhood depression
3. Recreational drug use
4. Malnutrition, particularly deficiencies in nutrients such as folic acid, iron, and Omega-3

In one of the author's conversations with a General Practitioner during a later episode abroad, an important discussion emerged around the role of nutritional imbalances. Deficiencies in iron, folic acid, and Omega-3 were noted as factors that may influence brain function and mental health. While these deficiencies are not regarded as direct causes of schizophrenia, they may contribute to the worsening of symptoms during an active episode or relapse.

In the author's opinion, it may also be useful to be mindful of prolonged social media consumption and extended use of headphones or ear-pods, as these activities can act as frequent sources of stimulation.

While such behaviours do not cause schizophrenia, they may exacerbate symptoms in some individuals by affecting dopamine regulation and concentration. Similar caution may apply to excessive consumption of other stimulants such as caffeine, smoking, and alcohol, particularly when used persistently or without moderation.

CHAPTER THREE

The Symptoms

The common symptoms of schizophrenia include delusions and hallucinations. Delusions basically mean holding true to a version, statement, or belief even when there is evidence available to the contrary. Hallucinations can be auditory or sensory. Auditory hallucinations are often characterised by the experience of noise in the head, as if someone is speaking, communicating, or instructing you to do something. Sensory hallucinations can sometimes be perceived with open eyes, even when nothing of that sort exists in external reality. In this context, sensory hallucinations refer to seeing things that do not actually exist.

Another characteristic that may occur during a prolonged episode of schizophrenia is extreme exhaustion, often associated with lack of sleep, inadequate water intake, and reduced food consumption, which can contribute to catatonia. Catatonia is a motor condition in which a person may either move erratically or not move at all. In cases where catatonia is associated with severe exhaustion, it is common to have very limited motor movement. Even getting up to fetch a glass of water can seem daunting, as the level of physical exhaustion can be that severe.

Other positive symptoms may include abnormal speech patterns and abnormal motor movements. Negative symptoms can include social withdrawal, poor hygiene, and lack of concentration.

CHAPTER FOUR

The Guardrails

In order to achieve remission, there is often an entire team of professionals and family members (care-givers as presumed Nominated Representatives in the absence of nomination) involved in the process of care. However, patient involvement should be paramount. If a patient is kept out of most decisions and does not fully understand the diagnosis, then it may indicate the need for systemic change.

The author would describe the following as guardrails within the Indian mental health scenario in the event of an episode of schizophrenia, or for that matter, other mental health spectrum conditions.

1. Psychiatrist and Psychologist

A psychiatrist is trained primarily in medical intervention, while a psychologist is trained in therapeutic listening and engagement. Psychiatrists hold medical degrees and can prescribe medication, whereas psychologists hold other university degrees and do not prescribe medication. In the author's observation, present-day care is often time-sensitive and incentive-driven, with a stronger emphasis on psychiatric intervention than on psychological support. While CBT (Cognitive Behavioural Therapy) forms part of the care process, psychologists may not always play as central a role as they ideally should.

Author's Note

PANSS (Positive and Negative Syndrome Scale) scores are used to assess the clinical state of an in-patient with schizophrenia. It is important that patients have memory and recollection of the interview questions, their responses, and the resulting scores, as these assessments influence the course of treatment. In the author's experience, this continuity of recollection does not always occur within the Indian mental health care context, particularly in some private care settings.

Consider a brain experiencing delusions or distorted beliefs, alongside a body that is severely exhausted due to lack of sleep, food, and water. In the author's lived experience, memory disruption began at the point of emergency sedation administered during admission, even prior to formal psychiatric evaluation. In the author's lived experience, this state was followed by high doses of anti-psychotics, injectables, and subsequent ECTs. This sequence placed the nervous system under significant strain.

In the author's lived experience, this sequence resulted in permanent memory loss of the in-patient stay, which directly affected the ability to participate meaningfully in subsequent assessments and consent processes. When such memory gaps occur, a patient may struggle to recall their own testimony during assessments; subsequent decisions may therefore be based on fragmented information, which can influence PANSS scores, and in some cases, lead to further intensification of interventions.

In this context, the author uses the term *spiral* to describe an observed pattern in her lived experience, where emergency sedation, subsequent ECTs, memory loss, heightened stress, and escalating interventions appeared to reinforce one another. This description is presented as a personal observation and not as an inevitable or universal trajectory.

The author has observed that while certain treatment protocols may resemble Western practices, comparable emphasis on patient rights and participation is not always evident within the Indian mental health care setting. In some cases, memory disruption may begin even before formal psychiatric evaluation when heavy sedation is administered at admission, leaving the patient unable to recall the circumstances or conversations that preceded subsequent interventions. This exclusion from one's own care process can have lasting psychological consequences.

The emotional impact of non-consensual treatment and prolonged memory gaps may persist long after discharge. Experiences of compromised autonomy can affect a patient's sense of adulthood and agency. In many instances, consents are signed by Nominated Representatives, who are often family members, sometimes with limited direct engagement with the patient.

The World Health Organization has recommended greater emphasis on community-based care over institution-based models. In the author's view, unless care models become more psychologist-led and centred on talk therapy, it may remain difficult to achieve true community-based care. Where primary intervention rests predominantly with psychiatrists, particularly in environments shaped by time and financial pressures, care may continue to remain institution-centric.

This author's note should be understood as a personal perspective informed by lived experience.

The Psychiatrist's Paradox

Psychiatric diagnosis is largely observation-based. When an episode is at its peak, symptoms such as sleep deprivation, blurred speech, tired eyes, trembling limbs, catatonia, delusional ideas, and the acceptance of "noises" in the head are noted. Everyday tasks such as personal hygiene, social interaction, and adherence to routine also form part of the assessment.

There are currently no tests that directly reveal neurotransmitter activity or accurately measure the concentration of misfiring dopamine. As a result, physical symptoms, behaviour, and mannerisms often provide the primary clinical clues. This can be frustrating for patients during an episode, and it can be equally challenging for psychiatrists. Routine blood tests are typically pathological in nature and are used to rule out factors such as nutritional deficiencies, including iron or folic acid, or blood-sugar imbalances.

Because of these limitations, psychiatrists often rely heavily on feedback from caregivers or nursing staff. This is where gaps in assessment can arise. Once the "noises" have subsided, discharge may be considered, even if the patient remains surrounded by ongoing triggers such as the strain of a restrictive ward, the fatigue of co-inhabiting with others in distress, or, in some cases, the continued presence of caregivers who are themselves experienced as primary triggers.

There are certain dopamine-related urine and blood tests, but these do not measure the neurotransmitter activity associated with mental imbalance, nor are they commonly used in day-to-day inpatient care. As a result, outward presentation, including appearance, calm tone, or politeness, may influence clinical impressions, but these alone do not necessarily indicate recovery or provide a complete diagnostic picture.

2. Nominated Representative (NR)

In case of an emergency, the nominated representative has the authority to sign consent and waiver forms on your behalf. In practice, family members are often presumed to be the NR, and the process of explaining patient rights may be limited, even during stable or remission states, particularly within the Indian context. You do have the right to change your NR to a trusted friend, another family member, or an NGO.

The author has explored this option. To do this, it is generally required to inform the current consulting psychiatrist. It is advisable to follow this up with an email to the psychiatrist and to immediate family members. For any new psychiatric consultation or emergency admission, the psychiatrist should be informed of who the NR is. Preferably, having the NR's visiting card or contact details readily available can be helpful, as emergency admissions are often sudden and leave little time to respond.

Ideally, the Nominated Representative should be registered with the Mental Health Review Board (MHRB), which is entrusted with the responsibility of overseeing the implementation of the Act at the state and district levels. However, at the time of writing this book, the existence and functioning of MHRBs remain uneven, and in many places, they are effectively absent. As a precaution, it may be useful to prepare a document stating the NR's name and the patient's wishes and have it notarised to provide additional legal weight. The author is considering doing this and combining NR nomination with an Advance Directive (AD).

Author's Note

The author feels that the NR becomes a necessary presence during emergencies. With limited understanding of procedures and the ailment, it is common for the NR to sign waivers and consent forms for interventions such as ECTs, which, in the author's lived experience, can contribute to the spiral discussed earlier. In the author's view, it is acceptable to refuse or delay invasive procedures when they are suggested early on.

The focus, in the author's opinion, should be on grounding the patient, which may include light oral sleep aids, oral anti-psychotics, adequate nutrition, and hydration. However, in practice, care can sometimes turn into a race against time, where the patient begins to lose grounding instead of regaining it. This can result in a loss of autonomous participation by the patient, with the NR effectively acting as a proxy.

Between the NR and the psychiatrist, most decisions are then taken on behalf of the patient in India. This situation, in the author's opinion, requires course correction and a shift in mindset towards longer-term, holistic care. A residual impact for the patient, particularly when permanent memory loss and aggressive treatments are involved, can be a profound loss of trust in the care process and, at times, in the NR as well.

Difference Between Loss of Grounding and Being Delusional

(This is the author's interpretation.)

Delusional episodes can make a person temporarily believe in other-worldly ideas. At times, one may feel like a victim of an external force, and at other times, feel as though they have overpowered it. A person may hear what sounds like a revolution, see flashes of the past, or perceive God-like figures, either internally or with open eyes, as hallucinations. This state is referred to here as delusion.

However, while a person is delusional, there is still memory and a degree of awareness of what is happening. These experiences can later be recollected and worked through using talk therapy and affirmations. A sense of personal identity remains intact. Reactions still feel owned. The person is present, even though perception is altered.

Loss of grounding, in the author's lived experience, emerges differently. When ECTs are administered in close succession during an already strained state, the mind can begin to lose its reference points. Reflexes may become defensive, guarded, or agitated, not necessarily from the illness itself, but from confusion and fear.

This is where the author observes a critical breakdown. Defensive responses may be misread as aggression. That aggression may then be interpreted as worsening psychosis. The response, in turn, is often further sedation or additional ECTs.

What may begin as a delusional state that could have been managed becomes a broader loss of grounding, not due to disease progression alone, but due to misinterpretation and cumulative over-intervention.

3. Caregiver

In the Indian context, the term "caregiver" is often used. The author personally feels that this term can induce a sense of loss of independence and disability. For this reason, the author does not prefer the term caregiver being used in her context.

At times, for individuals with mental health conditions, family members themselves can act as triggers, through no fault of their own. Typically, the primary co-inhabitant on whom the patient is financially dependent is presumed to be the caregiver. It is also usually presumed that the caregiver and the Nominated Representative are the same, unless stated otherwise, and this role is most often assigned to a family member.

However, in the author's opinion, family dynamics should be taken into account when such presumptions are made. Where concerns exist, and where they are operational, the Mental Health Review Board (MHRB) should be engaged for approval of the Nominated Representative, particularly during a first episode, when insight may be limited and erosion of consent can occur more easily.

4. Hospitals

Hospitals and the treating team are entrusted with the responsibility of upholding and practically implementing the Act, and of working in accordance with its provisions. However, in the author's lived experience within private care in India, the focus has often appeared to be on time-sensitive outcomes rather than on holistic recovery.

In the author's experience, the conditions that give rise to what is described earlier as a *spiral* emerged during both episodes of private care in India. The author believes that this progression could have been avoided had grounding been prioritised as a primary objective from the outset. Instead, a combination of presumed loss of capacity during emergency admissions, override of patient consent through the Nominated Representative, and emphasis on rapid stabilisation appeared to shape the course of care.

In this context, the author experienced that the loss of grounding was exacerbated rather than mitigated, which then made it easier to conclude that the patient lacked capacity. This, in turn, reinforced further exclusion of the patient from decision-making. From the author's perspective, stabilisation and grounding were not treated as front-line aims, and the resulting escalation intensified the very conditions used to justify continued override of consent.

This account reflects the author's lived experience within Indian private care. The author remains open to exploring public health care settings in India to assess whether differences exist in approaches to treatment, patient participation, and the practical upholding of patient rights.

5. Police

Police involvement may be required during emergency admissions where reasonable physical restraint becomes necessary. In the author's opinion, such situations are better handled through the presence of law enforcement rather than through the immediate administration of heavy sedative injections by hospital staff, particularly prior to psychiatric examination.

From the author's perspective, when sedation is required at the point of emergency admission, a lighter and preferably oral sleep aid may be less invasive and place less strain on the nervous system. In contrast, emergency provisions combined with injectable sedation at this stage, in the author's lived experience, marked the beginning of rights erosion and the spiral discussed earlier.

Wherever possible, the author believes that patients should be allowed to contact the police or speak with officers during in-patient stays if they feel their rights are being compromised. The ability to communicate, recall events, and retain lived memory and recollection matters.

All for lived memory and recollection!

6. Government and Legal Framework

The Mental Healthcare Act (MHCA), 2017 is a significant step in the right direction. The Act is intended to be patient-centric, as it should be. However, due to gaps in implementation and the limited existence of quasi-governing bodies such as the Mental Health Review Board (MHRB) at the state and district levels, there are evident and critical shortcomings, with limited avenues for timely redressal in cases of rights violations.

The open interpretation of emergency provisions and the extent of influence exercised by the Nominated Representative are areas within the Act that remain insufficiently defined and can be impairing for the patient. In the author's experience, this can create a sense of having lost the right to function as an autonomous adult.

Drafting and finalising an Advance Directive (AD) is also not straightforward. The absence of accessible authorities to register ADs, resistance from some psychiatrists, and procedural requirements such as witness attestation or notarisation can place an additional and often unnecessary burden on the patient. In the absence of supportive infrastructure, the Advance Directive can appear to function more as a placeholder than as an active and enforceable component of the Act.

7. Lawyers

Under the MHCA, 2017, a patient should be made aware of their legal rights, including the availability of free legal aid, by institutions or hospitals. Wherever possible, and in cases of perceived rights violations, the patient should be allowed to speak with a lawyer during in-patient care.

8. Employers

In the author's opinion, there are not enough open conversations about mental health in society. With growing concerns around mental health, it is imperative that employers come forward to encourage disclosure, provide insurance coverage, and offer flexible work arrangements that function practically beyond what is written in contracts.

Financial independence and stability are especially important for individuals living with mental health conditions. This is particularly relevant in the Indian context, where government subsistence or social security support for such disabilities is either absent or negligible.

CHAPTER FIVE

The Emergency Case Scenario in India

As per the Mental Healthcare Act (MHCA), 2017, emergency provisions may be invoked for a period of up to **72 hours from the time of admission. During this period, ECT is prohibited,** and the primary objective is meant to be stabilisation and grounding of the patient. In practice, however, emergency admissions are often invoked instead of calmer, assisted admissions. In the author's lived experience, families may prefer invoking emergencies, sometimes accompanied by heightened confrontation. In the author's case, this was the reality.

As stated earlier, in the author's lived experience, the spiral of memory loss began with the administration of sedative injections at the time of emergency admission, even before a psychiatric evaluation was conducted and prior to the subsequent administration of ECTs. This sequence resulted in treatment becoming largely centred around the Nominated Representative and the psychiatrist, with minimal scope for personal care, compassion, or patient participation.

This spiral can give the appearance that the patient's condition is deteriorating, when in reality the patient has lost grounding. There is often little emphasis on grounding the patient brought in under emergency provisions or enabling meaningful participation in decisions regarding the future course of treatment. In the author's view, this approach does not align with the spirit or intent of the MHCA, 2017.

Author's Note

In some cases, the Nominated Representative or family may panic, and exaggerated claims about the patient's condition can be presented to doctors. These claims are often accepted as true, even when the patient has no recollection of the events described or no opportunity to respond. In many cases, family members themselves may act as triggers, and their statements, in the author's opinion, should not singularly determine the future course of treatment.

The author also believes that what may be described as a *payer paradox*, where the individual controlling finances holds disproportionate influence, plays a role in such situations. Decisions may be taken while the patient lies heavily sedated, unable to participate or consent. In the author's view, the **emergency provision is among the most misused and misapplied sections of the Act.** In such circumstances, it becomes relatively easy to establish perceived harm to self or others, thereby invoking emergency provisions and setting the spiral in motion. It has also been observed by the author that many emergency admissions occur at night, when scrutiny and resistance are lower.

Through this book, the author requests those in positions of authority to consider more rigorous documentation requirements when invoking emergency provisions. The author further believes that it should be mandatory, wherever feasible, for a **psychiatrist to personally attend the site and conduct a pre-examination, rather than relying on immediate forced sedation.**

In the author's lived experience, during the first episode in 2019, she was attending office the day prior to admission. She was unaware of the ailment at the time and was severely confused, sleep-deprived, and lacking adequate food and water. Living away from family, she was alone in a hotel room when the emergency intervention occurred, with her mother arriving earlier that morning.

According to the author's recollection, three female hospital staff members entered the room, physically restrained her, and administered an injection without prior examination. She recalls being dragged barefoot to the ambulance. Upon arrival at the hospital, she was woken from sedation and again moved barefoot through the premises. This marks the last clear memory before prolonged memory loss ensued.

The author recalls seeing her mother observing from a distance as this occurred. The author experienced this treatment as degrading and dehumanising and regards it as a violation of her human rights. In the author's understanding, hospital staff should not physically restrain or sedate a patient prior to psychiatric examination. While police may intervene to contain a situation in a civilian space outside hospital premises, the author questions the legality and ethics of similar actions being taken by hospital staff within the hospital context prior to evaluation.

CHAPTER SIX

Treatment Options During In-Patient Care

This is a non-exhaustive list of treatment options that may be offered during in-patient care, and in some cases, continued post-discharge as maintenance doses.

1. Oral Medications

In the author's view, oral medications are among the safer and more participatory approaches to treating an adult patient, as they allow for greater involvement and consent. A measured dosage of oral antipsychotics, suited to age and individual profile, along with oral sleep aids if required, can form part of treatment.

However, caution is necessary to distinguish between cultural differences, innate personality traits, and symptoms of the ailment itself. Prolonged or excessive exposure to certain medications can lead to side effects such as hypnic jerks and tardive dyskinesia, which may be distressing. Some oral medications are also known to raise prolactin levels in women, potentially affecting menstrual cycles and sexual health. In the author's experience, these effects warrant careful discussion with the psychiatrist around dosage, tapering, and long-term maintenance levels.

Other reported side effects include elevated blood sugar levels, weight gain due to increased appetite, and cardiovascular strain. Lifestyle balance, although difficult when circadian rhythms are disrupted, may help mitigate some of these effects. The author notes that milder alternatives may be available and should form part of a measured discussion when considering maintenance treatment.

From the author's perspective, when possible, daytime medication may allow metabolic activity and structured meals to better regulate appetite. Where night-time medication is prescribed, reducing caffeine intake later in the day may support sleep continuity and limit night-time binge eating. Among available options, this approach has felt like the lesser of several difficult trade-offs.

2. Long-Acting Injectables (LAIs)

These are antipsychotics administered in the form of injections, typically given every two to four weeks. They release medication gradually into the bloodstream. LAIs are generally used as an alternative to oral medications and are often prescribed to support treatment adherence.

Based on the author's understanding and observation, oral medications and long-acting injectables are usually not administered together as primary treatment options. LAIs can be a suitable alternative for individuals who are uncomfortable with daily oral medication. However, they tend to be relatively expensive in the Indian context.

3. Psychotherapy

Psychotherapy is another term for talk therapy. It can be offered individually, in groups, or with family members where relational dynamics require attention. This can be a useful space to discuss matters concerning the patient, particularly in one-on-one sessions. However, if a patient is delusional during psychotherapy, this should not be held against them, and efforts should be directed towards gently restructuring thought patterns. In the author's opinion, psychotherapy should be given greater importance in the care of schizophrenia.

CBT (Cognitive Behavioural Therapy) is a subset of psychotherapy that focuses on recognising self-deprecating thoughts and replacing them with more constructive affirmations, with the aim of improving self-esteem and emotional regulation.

Author's Note

Due to the memory loss spiral described earlier, the author has no recollection of the psychotherapy sessions during both treatments in India. From the author's perspective, it is difficult to understand the value of such sessions when there is no memory or recall of them. These sessions are intended to bring about long-term changes in thought patterns and can be highly beneficial for patients in crisis. However, in the author's experience within the Indian mental health care context, they often appeared to function as a procedural requirement rather than a meaningful therapeutic engagement. This is the author's opinion.

These sessions also influence treatment dynamics, even when the patient is not grounded while being delusional during such spirals. In the author's view, it feels unfair to base treatment decisions on psychotherapy sessions conducted without the patient's meaningful participation, especially when the patient is unable to ask questions or seek clarification. Even if such participation technically occurred, the author questions how much could realistically be remembered.

In the context of memory loss, responses given during these sessions may also influence PANSS scores, which are then used to assess clinical progress. When a patient is unable to recall conversations, reflect, or cognitively integrate the session, these assessments can show a perceived slow improvement or perhaps even a decline initially. This, in turn, may justify further aggressive interventions. In the author's experience, a tool that is intended to support cognitive improvement and recovery can, under these conditions, become procedural and transactional rather than therapeutic.

In the author's lived experience, memory was intact up until the point of emergency hospitalisation, with the onset of the spiral beginning after the administration of sedative injections and continuing ECTs. The resulting memory loss prevented a return to grounding and meaningful participation in care, effectively rendering the author de facto incapacitated. The consent for treatment never reverted to the patient throughout the stay for both the episodes in India. In the author's view, this outcome runs contrary to the intent and spirit of the Mental Healthcare Act (MHCA), 2017, which emphasises capacity, participation, and patient-centric care.

The author's experience during the third episode abroad was different. No injectables were administered, and treatment involved only oral medications. The care felt more holistic, with ECG monitoring and regular blood tests. The author was able to participate in decision-making and refused ECTs. Although the duration of hospitalisation was longer and the oral dosage felt higher than necessary in the author's opinion, ECTs were not imposed, and memory and personal continuity were preserved. Even where consent was limited, it mattered.

There were group CBT sessions, laughter therapy, and art-based sessions. The author felt hesitant participating in group settings and requested individual one-on-one sessions with psychologists to process delusional emotions. This request, however, was not accommodated.

4. Electroconvulsive Therapy (ECT)

ECT involves the administration of controlled electrical impulses to the brain to induce brief, medically monitored seizures. It is believed to alter brain chemistry, and in some cases, promote neuroplastic changes. ECT is administered under general anaesthesia in controlled clinical settings. Reported short-term side effects may include headache, muscle aches, nausea, and a temporary rise in blood pressure. More serious reported side effects can include memory impairment, including long-term or permanent memory loss, as well as cardiac rhythm disturbances.

Author's Note

The author believes that ECT should not be used as an early or fallback treatment when a spiral has already been initiated and the patient's grounding and participation are diminishing. In the author's opinion, ECT should not function as a front-line intervention, as is often perceived in the Indian context, but rather be reserved as a last-resort option.

This is especially important in cases where there is a prior history of significant or permanent memory gaps, which, in the author's lived experience, is not uncommon. Under such circumstances, the use of ECT may further impair grounding and participation rather than restore them.

In the author's view, these treatment options work best when sequencing prioritises grounding and participation, rather than speed or escalation.

5. Repetitive Transcranial Magnetic Stimulation (rTMS)

Repetitive Transcranial Magnetic Stimulation (rTMS) is a non-invasive procedure that stimulates brain cells by generating a magnetic field over specific areas of the brain. It does not require anaesthesia and is typically administered in an outpatient setting.

Although rTMS has been widely studied for depression, research into its effectiveness for schizophrenia, particularly for negative symptoms and auditory hallucinations, is still ongoing. It has been used in certain cases as an adjunctive treatment.

The author does not have first-hand experience with this treatment option.

CHAPTER SEVEN

Discharge Planning Checklist and Treatment Post Discharge

Discharge Planning Checklist

This checklist is largely based on the author's experience of hospitalisation abroad, as there are no lived memories of in-patient treatment in India.

The checklist includes steps that may be considered prior to discharge, during the observation period.

1. Progress Update

Speak with the consultant psychiatrist and the psychologist to understand progress and the overall clinical assessment. In some cases, repeated ECTs or injectables may be advised post-discharge, particularly where non-adherence to oral medication has been observed. Such decisions are often influenced by living arrangements and behaviour leading up to discharge.

2. Maintenance Dose Discussion

Be open and candid when discussing maintenance dosage post-hospitalisation, as well as any future tapering plan. Dosages are often adjusted closer to maintenance levels near the time of discharge.

3. Tenure of Treatment

Have an upfront conversation about the expected duration of treatment. Initial episodes may allow for systematic tapering, and with holistic care, it may be possible to come off medication. With progressive or recurrent episodes, this can become a more difficult discussion. But let's not lose hope. Even if coming off medication entirely is not possible, a balanced life may help achieve a minimal maintenance dose and longer periods of remission. So, let's stay hopeful and optimistic, especially after an episode. Always!

4. Medication Preferences

Clearly state preferences regarding monotherapy or dual therapy for maintenance. If there is a preference for antipsychotics that are lighter on metabolism or reproductive health, raise this for discussion. Such options do exist. These are often slower-acting, daytime medications that may be suitable for maintenance, though not necessarily for stabilisation during an active episode. Be candid during these discussions. It is a fundamental right to be informed. Exercise it.

And yes, after an episode and a ward or hospital stay, **rest, process, and recharge**. Take as much time as you need. Just Rest! Rest! Rest! Give your sleep time to stabilise. Use sleep aids if necessary to establish a routine. Start light exercise such as yoga or walking. Eat well. And just relax.

This isn't the worst thing that could have happened. Watch less television and limit screen time, especially if ECTs were administered in the recent past. Just relax! You've been through enough.

Treatment Post Discharge

Treatment post discharge typically includes continuing the prescribed maintenance dosage. It also involves regular touchpoints with the psychiatrist for ongoing assessment. In many cases, however, psychologist-led care and CBT are not included to the extent they should be, especially where there has been ECT-induced permanent memory loss. The emphasis often remains more on medication than on holistic care.

Psychiatric follow-ups may be conducted online or in person, though in-person consultations are preferable where feasible. These check-ins can be used to ask questions arising from in-patient care, discuss side effects, and explore alternative medication options or lifestyle modification techniques. That said, in private care settings in India, these sessions are often significantly overpriced for regular follow-up.

Some additional initiatives that patients may consider independently, outside hospital care and psychiatrist-led treatment post discharge, include:

1. **Planning a solo trip once ready:** This is something the author is currently doing. She took her first, of hopefully many, solo trips to Jim Corbett National Park in February 2026 and had a memorable experience.
2. **Joining a support group, online or in person:** This remains exploratory for the author at present.
3. **Stabilising relationships with family:** If family members are a source of strength, that is valuable. Where there is limited understanding within the immediate or extended family, it may be necessary to draw boundaries without carrying negative emotion. Pent-up emotions can spiral into complications later. Maintaining distance, where possible, and protecting one's peace can be an important part of recovery.

CHAPTER EIGHT

My Consent

Under the Mental Healthcare Act, the emergency provision allows temporary suspension of consent for a limited duration. However, in the author's experience, what follows the emergency period can be far more concerning. Once emergency provisions are invoked, the presumption of the patient's consent often continues to be treated as interchangeable with that of the Nominated Representative, even after the 72-hour emergency window has ended.

As discussed earlier, the **author experienced the onset of an induced spiral of memory loss following emergency sedation and subsequent aggressive treatment involving multiple modalities, including ECTs. This resulted in complete and permanent memory loss of the inpatient stay.In such a state, the patient is often presumed to be de facto incapacitated.** In the author's experience, the treatments that follow do not restore grounding but instead deepen disorientation, making it increasingly difficult for the patient to meaningfully participate or reclaim consent during the course of inpatient care.

With a brain seeking memory and context, and delusions that lack reference points for resolution, consent becomes effectively non-existent. Decisions are discussed primarily between the Nominated Representative and the treating team, while the patient remains at the receiving end of care without knowledge, recollection, or informed participation. The author observed this pattern far more prominently in India than in treatment settings abroad, where patient rights appeared to be more clearly protected and mental health law more consistently applied.

A particularly troubling aspect of this process is the reliance on **PANSS scores to guide future treatment decisions.** These assessments are conducted through interviews and observations at a time when the patient may already be **losing grounding and memory, which can exacerbate symptoms rather than reflect true clinical deterioration.** Psychotherapy and CBT sessions, which are intended to support cognitive insight and improvement, may under such circumstances inadvertently contribute to further escalation of treatment rather than recovery.

In the author's lived experience, memory loss began prior to the administration of ECTs and continued thereafter, including during the period immediately following the expiry of the emergency provision. **This pattern was observed in both inpatient admissions in India.** As a result, consent was effectively presumed absent throughout the hospital stay, particularly in situations where family dynamics were complex or strained. The author experienced this as a gradual erosion of adult autonomy, creating a sense of having one's rights removed without ever being formally assessed or declared incapacitated.

CHAPTER NINE

Debunking Myths Around Patients with Schizophrenia in the Remission Phase

Remission is the phase in which, at a prima facie level, the patient has returned from hospitalisation and is maintained on a relatively lower dosage of medication. During this phase, the patient is often attempting to piece together a disrupted sense of identity and reintegrate into society.

However, remission does not imply the absence of difficulty. **Residual effects may still be present, not in the form of active psychotic symptoms, but as emotional and psychological consequences of the episode itself, and in some cases, of non-consensual treatments or prolonged ward stays. These may manifest as depression, emotional vulnerability, reduced responsiveness to reciprocal emotions, social withdrawal, and limited concentration or motivation, to name a few.** Remission is not the same as recovery, nor does it imply the absence of the ailment. The risk of relapse remains.

It is important to acknowledge that the experience of an episode is profoundly painful. **Delusional beliefs, combined with severe deprivation of sleep, food, and water, are real and debilitating,**

particularly for individuals living alone. Episodes can last from days to months. In the author's case, they have extended over several months. Being in such a prolonged and near-vegetative state is deeply distressing. What often follows, however, is treatment marked by limited understanding and a lack of compassion, depending on the care setting.

In the Indian context, the presence of permanent memory loss can further complicate recovery and continuity of care. From the author's perspective, the treatment trajectory may feel disjointed from a long-term standpoint. The patient may feel as uninformed and disoriented at the time of emergency admission as at discharge. Post-discharge conversations around symptom understanding and emotional processing are often limited. Psychiatric follow-ups, particularly in private care settings, tend to be time-constrained and costly, which can leave patients feeling unheard and unsupported.

This section attempts to debunk some common myths about patients with schizophrenia in the remission phase. Often, you would not know they are around you unless you consciously notice certain behaviours during periods of withdrawal. These behaviours may come across as attitude issues or personality traits.

What is often missed, however, is that beneath this exterior is someone who is recovering and adjusting to being brought back to memory, trying to retrain her brain on everyday tasks like working on spreadsheets, all while feeling drowsy on a maintenance dose of medication. And just when she might reach for a cup of coffee to stay alert, she cannot — because caffeine can induce insomnia when combined with certain antipsychotic medications.

1. Aggressive

Patients with schizophrenia are not typically aggressive, despite the fact that certain medications can induce agitation. Behaviour is often influenced by the environment in which the person is placed. In social settings where the individual feels respected and safe, aggression is usually not observed.

2. Social Withdrawal

Yes, people with this ailment may prefer to stay withdrawn and speak less. However, if a conversation is initiated and they are made to feel comfortable, they often come out of their shell and engage, not necessarily about the ailment but in general.

3. Being Dumb or Slow Acting

Patients with schizophrenia are often perceived as slow or cognitively impaired. In reality, what is commonly observed is psychomotor slowing, which can result from certain procedures, heavy medication, or prolonged hospitalisation. When not adequately balanced with psychotherapy and cognitive support, this slowing can begin to resemble peripheral cognitive difficulties. This imbalance becomes especially pronounced in situations where CBT is ineffective or impossible due to ECT-triggered memory loss.

In the author's opinion, ECT functions largely as a temporary intervention and may carry more drawbacks than benefits, particularly when used repeatedly. While it may help in reversing an acute episode, it does not necessarily support long-term cognitive integration. Over time, repeated episodes, aggressive treatments, and prolonged loss of grounding can contribute to a perceived or real decline in cognitive functioning.

Overall, patients with this ailment are often creative, introspective, and in need of personal space. They are not inherently slow or unintelligent. Where slowing or cognitive dulling is observed, the author believes it is more often a consequence of repeated episodes, misaligned treatments, or inadequate rehabilitation rather than a defining feature of the illness itself.

4. Speech

Speech may be altered due to medication effects, but it is generally well balanced when maintenance doses are kept low and aligned with factors such as gender profile, metabolism, and overall health.

5. Self-Confidence

Self-confidence is often very low after an episode, but it can gradually improve with social support and appropriate psychotherapy, including CBT.

6. Lack of Motivation

Lack of motivation often stems from physiological side effects rather than the ailment itself. When the maintenance dose is balanced in a way that the body can adapt to, motivation may gradually return. A pep talk from someone familiar can go a long way. Periodic check-ins with trusted aides, especially when living independently, can also help restore motivation.

7. Asexual Tendency

This is a subjective and difficult area to articulate. In the author's experience, certain medications can interfere significantly with sexual functioning, affecting intimacy and attraction. These effects are often related to medication strength rather than the ailment itself. There are alternative options that may be considered at the maintenance stage. Some of these are slower acting and therefore less commonly used as first-line treatments, but they may have a lesser impact on sexual well-being.

CHAPTER TEN

FOOD FOR THOUGHT

In this chapter, the author explores certain caveats and terms across the treatment spectrum that may warrant reconsideration in the Indian context, particularly in relation to how patient rights are interpreted and how the ailment itself is treated. This section is intended as an open forum for reflection and discussion.

1. Necessity of Nominated Representative (NR) under MHCA 2017

Not all countries operate with a system of a Nominated Representative. While having someone to support decision-making can be beneficial where trust exists, the question remains: what if a patient does not wish to relinquish decision-making rights at all? There should be a provision within the Mental Healthcare Act, 2017 **to allow a patient to opt out of appointing an NR.** The role **should not be mandatory by default.** Instead, the primary focus should be on grounding the patient and enabling day-to-day participation in their own care.

In practice, the presence of an NR can become borderline exploitative, particularly because many individuals with mental health conditions come from estranged or complex family structures and may not have a reliable trust group. In such situations, consent begins to feel less voluntary and more coerced. It becomes easier to prioritise short-term stabilisation through invasive procedures rather than investing time and effort into grounding the patient and supporting long-term recovery. An NR should not be automatic, dominant, or overriding when a patient is capable of grounding and participation.

At this point, the author finds the discussion circling back to a deeper concern: **does the system genuinely prioritise grounding?** In the author's lived experience, the memory loss spiral begins at the point of emergency admission, with the administration of heavy sedative injections, often at night, even before subsequent treatments such as ECTs are introduced and before examination by a psychiatrist in emergency scenarios which is very loosely outlined in the MHCA and is discussed in detail later. Structurally, grounding does not appear to be prioritised. Instead, disorientation becomes functionally useful.

Importantly, at the time of emergency, the patient does not necessarily lack memory or comprehension. However, following admission, particularly in private care settings in India, grounding begins to erode while the patient remains delusional. This erosion then becomes the basis for NR override and exclusion from participation, under the presumption of de facto loss of capacity for the duration of inpatient care.

The patient is gradually reduced to what feels like a talking experiment, engaging in interviews and sessions without any recollection of them, while these very interactions are used to justify further aggressive treatments within the spiral. Imagine a brain searching desperately for memory and context in the midst of injectables, high-dose oral medications, ECTs, and CBT sessions, all of which are paid for, yet experienced as a complete blur.

When the author uses the term "talking experiment," it is meant quite literally. During wakeful hours, the patient speaks and responds, but retains no memory of these interactions due to invasiveprocedures. This is a serious concern. In the author's case, this phase extended for nearly a month during the first hospitalisation.

It is also important to distinguish this experience from anaesthesia-induced sedation used for a specific surgical procedure over a defined time frame. The two are not comparable. Here, the concern is about days or weeks of lost memory while the patient is conscious, ambulatory, and communicative. PANSS scores generated during these periods of memory loss are then used to justify further aggressive treatment and to perpetuate the presumption of incapacity.

In the author's view, this **induced memory loss spiral operates as a loophole within the emergency provisions of the Act.** It allows patient consent and participation to be overridden long after the emergency period has ended, particularly in private care settings in India, by maintaining a state of de facto incapacitation.

2. Advance Directive (AD)

In the absence of effective safeguards, the Advance Directive often becomes a necessary but imperfect tool. An Advance Directive is a document through which a patient records preferences for future mental health care while they have capacity. **Under the Mental Healthcare Act, 2017, an AD is intended to guide treatment decisions when a patient is assessed as lacking capacity. Where capacity is retained, the patient's current autonomy and consent are meant to prevail, irrespective of the existence of an AD, particularly once the 72-hour emergency period has ended.**

In the author's understanding, the AD is meant to act as a counterbalance to automatic reliance on the Nominated Representative, especially outside emergency provisions. In theory, this preserves patient autonomy. In practice, however, retaining capacity does not always translate into meaningful participation during inpatient care in India. The author raises this as a systemic concern rather than an allegation of intent.

A template for an Advance Directive is provided in the Appendix 4. In the author's experience, drafting an AD itself can be a taxing process. **Even in a stable, non-hospitalised state, psychiatrists may require additional psychological assessments to certify fitness before acknowledging or supporting the creation of an AD.** As of November 2025, despite not being hospitalised and functioning independently, the author was advised to undergo a series of psychological assessments to "prove fitness," and a fitness certificate was declined. This illustrates how difficult self-directed care planning can become when implementation of the law is inconsistent and incentive-driven.

Registering an Advance Directive presents further barriers. The process typically requires either **attestation by two witnesses for a**

deeply personal document or notarisation. Additionally, Mental Health Review Boards (MHRBs) are not operational in many districts, making it nearly impossible to formally register or file ADs with the government, even several years after the Act's enactment.

The deeper concern arises when comprehension is considered compromised, particularly in contexts where over-treatment and induced spirals of memory loss occur. In such situations, grounding the patient and adhering to the Advance Directive becomes increasingly difficult. Residual autonomy is lost, and decision-making often shifts entirely to the Nominated Representative or the presumed payer. The patient is relegated to the background.

In the author's view, this outcome stems from a system that does not prioritise grounding. Stabilisation should begin with sleep regulation, oral medications suited to individual profiles to minimise blackouts and preserve memory, adequate nutrition and hydration, hygiene, access to fresh air, and daily talk-based engagement to arrive at consented procedures. Forced ECTs administered to a body already deprived of sleep, water, and nutrients undermine this process.

While such treatment patterns may produce short-term clinical outcomes, they often leave behind lasting psychological consequences rooted in coercion, loss of consent, and significant memory gaps. Over time, repeated experiences of coercion can erode a patient's sense of safety and agency. The author notes that while clinical symptoms may be addressed, the experience of oppression can persist long after discharge.

3. The Concept of Capacity

As discussed earlier, capacity is highly subjective from an assessment standpoint. **The Mental Healthcare Act, 2017 defines capacity as the ability to understand information relevant to a treatment decision and to be aware of the reasonably foreseeable consequences of that decision.**

If the person is not capable of understanding language, then he or she should be explained to and communicated with using simplified language or appropriate gestures. However, **the condition is rarely this severe in acute psychosis. Yet, in practice, this safeguard is often not followed.**

In the author's two admissions in India, she walked out of the hospitals with no recollection of discharge, no recollection of the name of the ailment, and no meaningful long-term integration from CBT.

While delusional, an episode by itself does not necessarily cause memory loss unless invasive sedation or intensive treatments are administered. Prior to such interventions, a patient may retain the capacity to understand, comprehend, respond, and participate in their care.

Capacity remains one of the **most open-ended concepts under the Mental Healthcare Act, 2017**. In the author's view, any determination of lack of capacity should be supported by adequate documentation. **Failing this, capacity ought to be presumed.**

It is imperative that, at the time of capacity assessment, the patient is grounded, and that **the impact of administered procedures, including sedation and ECT, is clearly documented in relation to their effect on memory, orientation, and capacity.**

Author's Note

In the author's lived experience, high doses of antipsychotics were administered daily, along with multiple injectables within a short period and ECTs on alternate days during an episode in India. The author has no memory of the inpatient stay. Based on the known sedative impact of these invasive procedures, it can reasonably be understood that the author was unconscious or significantly disoriented for much of this period. These same conditions then informed PANSS assessments, which in turn led to further aggressive treatment.

The author remembers seeing charges for sanitary pads in the billing summary, even though hospitals are supposed to maintain a supply of hygiene products. However, the author does not remember changing pads or being administered injectables in the pelvic area in a dignified setting.

Sadly, this is the emotional load the author carries on a daily basis, and it refuses to die down.

4. The Emergency Provision

As discussed earlier, the spiral often begins with sedation administered during emergency admission, when loss of capacity is presumed and subsequently eroded through further invasive procedures. This process closes the loop as **declining or marginally improving PANSS scores** are misinterpreted in the context of treatment overload, sustained sedation, and repeated interventions. There are **no clear guidelines on who may initiate an emergency admission. A psychiatrist may, on the basis of a declared emergency, sign an order to have the patient brought in without any examination at the point of apprehension.** Hospital authorities then execute this order, assuming control over the patient without involvement of civic authorities. This mechanism is used to **justify forceful sedation and a degrading mode of patient capture.** I use these terms deliberately, because the **lived experience of emergency admission in India often parallels that of a criminal arrest while being ill.**

Further, the Act does not clearly delineate safeguards governing institutional control during such emergencies, allowing hospital authorities to **assume coercive powers** in the absence of independent oversight. In the author's opinion, **sedation during an emergency should not be administered** to a body that is already stressed, sleep-deprived, or deprived of food and water. Instead, where clinically feasible, mild oral sleep aids should be preferred, so that the spiral of escalating intervention does not set in.

5. PANSS Scores

PANSS stands for the Positive and Negative Syndrome Scale. It is used to **measure the severity of symptoms in schizophrenia, including positive symptoms, negative symptoms, and general psychopathology symptoms.**

These assessments are usually conducted at the time of admission, or shortly thereafter, to establish a baseline score, followed by periodic evaluations. **A lower PANSS score implies improvement.**

The scale includes items assessing positive symptoms, negative symptoms, and psychopathology features such as emotional, cognitive, and behavioural disturbances.

Author's Note

In the author's two treatment experiences, there was significant procedural overlap across different mental health establishments in different parts of the country. This pattern suggests systemic standardization, but also highlights how, in practice, consent overrides may become easier under loosely implemented safeguards.

In both instances, the spiral began with the administration of emergency sedatives. The condition of memory impairment was, in the author's experience, worsened following aggressive and non-consensual ECT.

Consider a system in which high-dose medication, long-term injectables, and ECT are administered within overlapping treatment windows. The cumulative sedative burden can significantly affect cognition. When memory retention is impaired for days at a time in the name of stabilization, the question arises: how reliable are subsequent psychiatric assessments?

If PANSS scores are calculated and CBT sessions conducted during periods of acute sedation and cognitive blunting, can the assessment truly reflect the patient's baseline mental state? Or does it reflect the aftermath of intensive intervention?

Most critically, the patient risks losing her narrative. Her testimony. Her right to remember her own words. Her own story.

In the absence of induced or treatment-related memory impairment, CBT may have greater long-term effectiveness. Delusional beliefs can be addressed with evidence-based dialogue, allowing for future self-recognition of symptoms.

Due to the highly transactional nature of mental healthcare treatment in India, these sessions become mere tick boxes and justifications for further escalation.

6. Mobile Phone

The Mental Healthcare Act, 2017 recognises the right to communication, including phone calls, subject to the reasonable norms of the establishment. Accordingly, and within hospital policies, it is not unreasonable to request that a patient's phone remain with them and be kept charged. This, however, is realistically possible only when the patient retains memory and is participating in treatment through consent rather than coercion.

Author's Note

During the author's treatment abroad, the phone was accessible at all times. While wires and chargers were not permitted, nurses charged the phone at designated office charging stations. This arrangement was inconvenient, but it ensured continuous access to communication throughout treatment. In contrast, such access was not available during treatment in India, alongside the loss of memory experienced there.

7. Legal Aid

Author's Note

During the author's admission abroad, a list of lawyers was made available at the time of admission. These consultations could be used to negotiate medication levels if they felt excessive. A separate list of lawyers was also available to request a hearing for release if the patient felt they were being detained beyond the required period. Such was the level of procedural precision. Nurses actively handed over these lists and informed patients of their rights.

In contrast, within the Indian context, there is no readily available list of lawyers provided at the time of admission. Based on the author's research, while mental health patients are legally entitled to free legal aid, access is not integrated into hospital systems. In practice, legal aid is routed through district and state Legal Services Authorities rather than hospital-based mechanisms, which explains the absence of a readily available list of mental-health-specific advocates at the time of admission.

This remains exploratory for the author, but engaging with a pro bono lawyer during a stable phase and explaining one's case history in advance may be helpful. Maintaining contact with such a lawyer and utilising their services in the event of an assisted or emergency admission may provide an added layer of support. Having a pre-established relationship allows the patient to seek assistance in negotiating medication schedules suited to their profile or in facilitating conversations around discharge once stability returns.

In addition, despite several years of psychiatric consultation in India, the author was never informed of the option to draft an Advance Directive. This contrast further highlights how patient rights are prioritised differently and warrants serious reflection. At the time of writing this book, the author's priority remains finalising the Advance Directive, while legal aid is being considered as a fallback option within the Indian context.

8. The Payer Paradox

Author's Note

One of the influencing factors during admission is what the author describes as the payer paradox. In many cases, the payer, who is often also the Nominated Representative, exercises significant influence over the direction of treatment in the absence of the patient's consent and awareness, particularly in private care settings in India that are both incentive-driven and time-sensitive.

Another dimension of this paradox is the emphasis on time efficiency. In such contexts, aggressive and mind-numbing procedures may be favoured to achieve short-term clinical outcomes, often overlooking the long-term psychological and physical impact these interventions can have. Treatment decisions can begin to feel payer-driven rather than patient-centred. In the author's opinion, the experience of care can differ markedly when the patient is financially independent and able to directly bear the cost of treatment.

An alternative route is the use of employer-provided health insurance for those who are employed. However, due to the stigma associated with mental health conditions, some patients may hesitate to utilise insurance coverage, as it can require greater disclosure than a simple fitness certificate. Despite this, disclosure can help maintain balance and transparency, particularly in cases of schizophrenia.

From the author's perspective, insurance coverage can also function as an additional checkpoint against overtreatment, as third-party involvement introduces greater documentation requirements and a clearer paper trail. For patients in India who have experienced aggressive or non-consensual treatment, using insurance may provide both financial relief and an added layer of accountability.

9. Longevity and Over-Treatment

A healthy, well-functioning body is a fundamental right. Some procedures and medications can leave long-lasting effects, even in situations where slower and less aggressive alternatives were available in terms of both time and resources. If you feel this way, as the author does, without going into the specifics of how aggressive treatments have affected quality of life or longevity, it may be worth raising these concerns with your psychiatrist and, where appropriate, seeking legal advice. As patients, access to free legal aid is available in India.

10. Access to Fresh Air and Humane Living Conditions

This concern is most relevant when a patient has recollection of their treatment and is an active participant in care. During admission in many Indian hospitals, access to fresh air or outdoor space is not permitted. While this may be attributed to urban constraints, alternatives such as community gardens within hospital premises, secured with appropriate safety measures, can and should be explored.

Access to fresh air, walking space, daylight, and the ability to form memories while in hospitals and wards are basic human needs. These elements contribute not only to physical well-being but also to dignity and psychological recovery.

11. Organic vs Non-Organic Psychosis

Organic psychosis refers to psychotic symptoms that arise secondary to an identifiable medical or neurological condition. This may include brain injury, infections, metabolic disturbances, endocrine disorders, or neurodegenerative conditions. Such presentations are often accompanied by fluctuating consciousness, cognitive impairment, or unstable vital parameters, and require thorough medical evaluation alongside psychiatric care.

Functional psychosis, sometimes referred to as primary psychosis, **does not have an immediately identifiable structural or medical cause and is largely diagnosed through clinical observation.** Vital parameters are typically stable, and cognition may remain intact outside of acute episodes. **Schizophrenia and related psychotic disorders fall within this category.**

Substance-induced psychosis represents a distinct and important category. Certain substances, including recreational drugs, can precipitate psychotic symptoms. In some cases, these symptoms resolve with abstinence and supportive care, while in others they may unmask or coexist with an underlying primary psychotic vulnerability.

The author wishes to open a broader discussion around the importance of differentiating between organic, functional, and substance-induced psychosis. Each has different implications for prognosis, treatment sequencing, and recovery. In the author's view, medical practitioners should approach these distinctions with care and respect, tailoring stabilisation and remission strategies to the underlying cause rather than applying uniform, aggressive interventions across all presentations.

12. Public Vs Private Care

Author's Note

For both episodes in India, the author was treated under private care and was dissatisfied with what felt like an aggressive, time-sensitive, and transactional approach. The author remains open to exploring the public healthcare system in India, while recognising that it has its own limitations, particularly during emergencies, where capacity constraints and demand across all strata of society often exceed supply.

That said, the author would consider voluntary admission during a future episode, preferably at an early stage of onset, in order to engage with the public healthcare system and assess whether patient rights may be better protected in a setting where financial considerations are not the primary driver.

In contrast, the author's treatment abroad took place within a public healthcare facility. While there were reservations regarding certain aspects of diagnosis and care, the author found reassurance in the fact that invasive procedures were not forced, and that the right to participation and memory were respected.

13. Kundalini Experiences and Psychosis: Where Confusion Arises

Author's Note

It is traditionally believed that day-to-day functioning of the body is influenced by chakras, or energy centres. There are said to be seven such centres, located at different points in the body, associated with various physical, emotional, and cognitive functions. These chakras are thought to be influenced by thoughts, actions, and lifestyle factors, including stress, exercise, and nutrition. In some belief systems, prolonged stress is considered a factor that can disrupt this internal balance, sometimes presenting in ways that resemble psychosis-like symptoms.

In such frameworks, individuals may report out-of-body, astral, or inwardly vivid experiences, described metaphorically as another set of eyes opening, the eyes of the mind. Experiences such as auditory or sensory perceptions and voices may be described in this context. As an author, the intent here is not to critique psychiatric practice or challenge clinical interpretations that may reject such explanations.

There remain areas of human experience and consciousness that medical science continues to explore. The author's request is simply that such experiences be approached with caution rather than immediate dismissal, and that any corrective or explanatory conversations occur while the patient retains memory and recollection. This allows the patient to process, contextualise, and reinterpret these experiences over time, or to seek medical help proactively in the future. Trust, in the author's view, is mutual and must operate as a two-way process.

When such experiences are met with aggressive treatment and result in permanent memory loss, significant emotional and psychological gaps can emerge. Without memory of discussions, explanations, or corrective framing, the patient is left without a reference point for course correction. This, in the author's experience, creates a long-term problem in mental healthcare: aversion to discussion combined with limited or absent recollection of therapeutic conversations. In the author's case, the diagnosis itself became clear only months after discharge, upon reading the discharge summary, reflecting the extent of memory loss during treatment.

To fellow patients who may hold similar notions or experiences, the author offers this reflection: such experiences need not be rejected outright, but they should be held lightly and examined alongside medical understanding. Physical and mental balance cannot be restored without the support of modern medicine, and acceptance of treatment is often necessary. However, mutual respect, dialogue, and informed cooperation should guide care, rather than aggressive and uninformed intervention.

14. Gender: Male vs Female Profiles and Dosage

Author's Note

In the author's opinion and lived experience, having been prescribed various antipsychotic medications over time before eventually identifying one that suited her metabolic and reproductive health, it became apparent that factors such as metabolism, hormonal profile, age, genetic predisposition, and vulnerability to certain side effects require careful consideration. In the author's case, this alignment was achieved only during treatment abroad, several years after initial medication exposure.

In the author's view, biological differences, including fat distribution and metabolic rate, can influence how medications are processed, particularly in women. This may warrant more cautious dosing during both in-patient treatment and maintenance phases. Certain antipsychotics are associated with pronounced hunger, weight gain, elevated prolactin levels affecting menstrual cycles, and sedation. These effects can increase physiological and psychological stress.

While some research acknowledges sex-based differences in response to antipsychotic medication, the author believes that gender-specific considerations are not yet adequately reflected in routine clinical practice. Greater emphasis on gender-informed research and prescribing may help improve tolerability, adherence, and long-term outcomes.

15. Sleep as a Primary Stabiliser

Sleep. I cannot stress this enough. Nothing is more important than a restful night's sleep. A disturbed sleep pattern is often the first indicator that a patient needs to self-monitor. If poor sleep stretches beyond a couple of days, accompanied by incessant thoughts, emotional distress, sudden loss of concentration, or appetite changes, it may signal the onset of an episode, even before more prominent symptoms such as hallucinations or delusions appear. This is especially relevant if you have a prior history of the illness.

Sleep disruption should therefore be taken seriously. Reaching out to your treating doctor early to address sleep, including short-term use or adjustment of sleep medication under medical guidance, may help stabilise symptoms. Monitoring closely over the next few days is important. If symptoms persist or escalate despite these measures, voluntary admission at an early stage may be a safer and more participatory option.

16. Medication Adherence vs Informed Refusal

Author's Note

Adhering to prescribed medication schedules is important, not only during in-patient care but also during the maintenance phase after discharge. At the same time, an episode should not automatically be presumed to indicate a lifelong, continuously recurring condition. With commitment to holistic mental and physical care, recovery beyond remission can be a possibility. For the author, this has felt like a distant possibility, but it remains a possibility nonetheless.

Especially after a first episode, it is important to have open conversations with the psychiatrist about tapering and the anticipated duration of treatment. Tapering should be gradual and carefully supervised, as abrupt discontinuation increases the risk of relapse.

As episodes recur, these conversations often become more complex, particularly after multiple episodes. In such cases, the focus may shift toward holistic care alongside gradual tapering to a dosage that is low enough to minimise side effects and allow meaningful day-to-day functioning, rather than complete discontinuation.

This section has been especially heavy to draft in the author's experience. While trying to process and analyse these open-ended questions, the author feels that no one involved across the spectrum, from patient to doctors to nominated representatives to the government, has the full picture or context. However, the patient is often at the receiving end of these gaps.

It becomes easy and convenient to induce a spiral and document loss of capacity. As a result of these psychological gaps and uninformed, out-of-consent treatments, six years after diagnosis, the author does not feel healed. *The author feels oppressed.*

Hence the name of the book, *The In(Complete) Arc*. From everyone's individual perspective, one may be informed, but collectively perhaps not. The arc remains incomplete, with an illusion of completion or recovery.

CHAPTER ELEVEN

Voluntary Admission and Early Self-Advocacy

As an author and a person with lived experience, I cannot stress this enough. Through observation, I have noticed that patients who opt for voluntary admission often demonstrate better prima facie insight. They are also more likely to be perceived by doctors as having insight, because once surface-level symptoms subside, clinicians largely rely on external behaviour to assess the persistence of symptoms. There is no objective measure, such as a real-time indicator of dopamine levels, to infer internal experience. In that context, cooperation, self-awareness, and voluntary engagement with care signal a great deal.

Voluntary admission, coupled with a focus on self-care, can therefore influence how treatment is approached. In the author's understanding of the Mental Healthcare Act, 2017, voluntary admission should not invoke emergency provisions. Emergency provisions are among the most delicate aspects of the Act, and when invoked, can set in motion spirals that lead to erosion of consent and patient participation.

Another significant pitfall relates to the role of the Nominated Representative, particularly where family ties are strained or where family members themselves are triggers. This is not uncommon among mental health patients in early or middle adulthood who continue to live with parents or siblings and remain financially dependent due to limited government support in India. In such circumstances, choice becomes constrained.

For those who do have the option, returning to work, regaining financial independence, and integrating back into daily life as early as possible can be an important form of self-advocacy and protection of autonomy.

CHAPTER TWELVE

Crisis Checklist

This section shifts focus back to the patient's perspective and outlines what a patient may consider doing differently at the onset of a crisis.

1. Seek Professional Help Early

Speak to a healthcare professional at the onset, especially if you have not slept for a couple of days. Where possible, state your preference for the initial form of treatment, such as hospitalisation versus home-based care, if feasible. The final decision will depend on the doctor's assessment of symptom severity and your living circumstances. In cases where family support is absent, hospitalisation may be safer for monitoring. At early stages, it can be difficult to distinguish between heightened internal thought activity and the emergence of voices, particularly during panic. If sleep, appetite, or concentration are significantly disturbed, or if persistent thoughts or voices emerge, seek professional help immediately.

2. Use Early Aversion and Grounding Techniques

At the earliest signs, try light grounding activities such as going for a short walk, focusing attention on fixed objects such as a light, wall hanging, or a picture of a deity as meditation techniques, hydrating adequately, and eating regular meals. These measures may help slow the pace of racing thoughts, even during an episode.

3. Engage Both Psychiatric and Psychological Support Early

Where possible, involve both a psychiatrist and a psychologist at an early stage.

4. Keep Key Documents Accessible

Ensure that details of your Advance Directive, Nominated Representative, and any legal support are readily available.

5. Avoid Emergency Invocation where Possible

Where feasible, attempt to avoid emergency provisions being invoked, as this can result in loss of consent and participation. Early recognition and timely voluntary presentation may help reduce the likelihood of emergency measures, particularly where family dynamics are strained or triggering.

Author's Note

In the author's lived experience, emergency admission was accompanied by physical coercion and forced sedation prior to psychiatric assessment, resulting in permanent loss of memory and grounding. This experience informs the author's emphasis on early voluntary engagement, where clinically appropriate.

6. Consider Voluntary Admission with Clear Preferences Stated

One approach that may help preserve participation is early acceptance and voluntary admission, accompanied by a clear written statement, ideally aligned with your Advance Directive. This may include stating that while you may be experiencing delusional symptoms, you retain grounding and are willing to work with clinicians. You may also state preferences regarding treatment sequencing, such as prioritising grounding and oral medication before more invasive interventions, subject to clinical judgment.

Where possible, arriving voluntarily at a time when psychiatrists are available may reduce the likelihood of interim measures being taken before assessment.

CHAPTER THIRTEEN

The Ordeal of Advance Directives in India

Author's Note

As recently as November 2025, my consulting psychiatrist advised me to undergo a series of psychological assessments solely for the purpose of drafting my own Advance Directive in my personal space. This was not in the context of returning to work, managing risk, or a post-hospitalisation review, but purely to determine my "fitness" to draft an Advance Directive, an instrument that exists precisely to protect autonomy during future periods of incapacity.

At the time, I was not hospitalised. I was consulting via teleconference, a mode of care that was charged at the same rate as an in-person consultation. I also had a documented history of prior psychiatric consultations conducted online. Despite this, incapacity appeared to be presumed, not assessed.

The stated justification for the refusal was that this was only our second meeting and that the consultation was conducted via teleconference. This reasoning raises a troubling question: if teleconsultation is deemed insufficient to recognise capacity, what is the ethical or professional basis for charging it at parity with in-person care? More importantly, how does the medium of consultation negate a legal presumption of capacity?

The insistence on additional assessments, in this context, directly impeded my fundamental right to draft and sign my own Advance Directive. This right flows not only from the provisions of the Mental Healthcare Act, 2017 but also from the broader protections of personal autonomy under the Constitution of India. It effectively transformed a right into a permission-based process, contingent not on evidence of incapacity but on institutional comfort.

Compounding this concern, both the hospital and the psychiatrist requested that I share my Advance Directive via WhatsApp rather than email to customer support, even though the document contained confidential and personal information. I considered this inconsistent with patient–psychiatrist confidentiality and against the spirit of the Mental Healthcare Act, 2017. No acknowledgment of receipt was provided, nor was there confirmation in the subsequent follow-up that the document had been read or considered.

I requested confirmation of receipt via email, but it never came through. In the process, I was asked to share the Advance Directive multiple times. I recall sending it three times and following up repeatedly, which increased my stress levels given my six-year medical history with mental health care. I found the experience deeply distressing.

Taken together, these actions do not reflect an excess of caution. They reflect a systemic inversion of principle: where capacity is no longer presumed unless disproven, but instead withheld until repeatedly certified. In such a framework, autonomy becomes procedural, fragile, and easily deferred.

This reflects, in the author's experience, a troubling side of private healthcare—where, in addition to assessments during remission, patient residential programs are presented as comprehensive care packages, even as fundamental legal agency may be subtly limited within an otherwise polished framework.

This also appears inconsistent with certain emergency practices the author has observed. In emergency situations, a psychiatrist may authorise the retrieval and sedation of a patient before any detailed examination. The patient may be physically restrained by nursing staff and administered sedatives before being transported to the hospital facility. In such circumstances, the author's experience has been that the memory spiral begins even before a formal examination takes place. This sequence, in practice, can become a highly convenient pathway around the emergency and capacity safeguards envisioned under the Mental Healthcare Act, 2017, which—without proper controls and countermeasures—may be applied loosely.

Yet, in contrast, capacity assessments via teleconference after multiple consultations appear to be considered insufficient. This becomes especially difficult to reconcile when the Advance Directive is being drafted privately in one's personal space without posing any external risk. Under the Mental Healthcare Act, 2017, capacity is presumed unless proven otherwise, even after hospitalisation. A patient may therefore participate in decisions regarding the trajectory of treatment within the hospital setting. In that light, the question arises: why should a patient be prevented from drafting their own Advance Directive in a non-hospitalised state?

Furthermore, the concerned psychiatrist repeatedly referred to evaluating "insight" into the ailment for the purpose of issuing a fitness certificate to draft the Advance Directive. However, the Mental Healthcare Act, 2017 refers to **capacity**, not insight. A patient may have impaired clinical insight due to treatment history or care circumstances, yet still retain decisional capacity.

In my own experience, the treatments resulted in permanent memory loss while leaving the lived memory of delusional experiences intact. Aggressive interventions erased the benefits of expensive CBT sessions that are intended to counter delusions and help build insight. After such treatment-related harm, the discussion returned once again to insight. I had to rely on discharge summaries and independent research to understand the nature of the ailment. On both occasions in India, I walked out of the hospitals with no lived memory of the admission, no recollection of the diagnosis, and no clear memory of the treatment team.

Caught between clinical caution and procedural convenience, one can begin to feel like a scapegoat from both sides—spoken about, decided for, and protected in theory, yet steadily erased in practice.

General Practice among Psychiatrists regarding assumptions of Emergency Provisions, Lack of Insight, and Rigorous Prescribing in a Field that is Largely Observational rather than Diagnostic

In practice, discussions around fitness often arrive pre-loaded with emergency contingencies. The language used tends to lean toward over-caution, signalling that capacity is assumed to be temporary and revocable.

I observed a recurring emphasis on emergency admission over controlled, voluntary conversations during this meeting. The language used often leaned heavily toward over-caution and rigorous prescribing, at times bordering on professional overreach.

During one teleconsultation, when I expressed my intention to change my Nominated Representative to a friend, the psychiatrist advised me to keep his (NR's) visiting card ready "in case of an eventuality" and suggested that he preferably sign my Advance Directive. Under the Mental Healthcare Act, 2017, no such requirement exists for a Nominated Representative to sign an Advance Directive.

More concerning was the implicit assumption that emergency provisions would inevitably be invoked in the future, accompanied by statements suggesting that "they would then do what they have to do." Such anticipatory framing erodes trust. It presumes lack of insight unless proven otherwise and leaves little room for alternate lawful pathways such as voluntary admission.

More importantly, this exposes the transactional nature of certain private care systems in India, particularly in mental health.

When patients lack independently researched information, they may be unable to discern these alternatives. The routine and premature invocation of emergency provisions, even at the level of discourse, reflects a worrying trend that risks normalising coercion over collaboration.

CHAPTER FOURTEEN

THE SPECTRUM

Mental health disorders often follow patterns that include self-neglect, low self-esteem, and complex family dynamics. An episode represents an active symptomatic state, while remission refers to the phase in which symptoms subside. Schizophrenia is a treatable condition, though there is no definitive cure. Many individuals are able to function close to baseline during remission, although certain treatment-related effects, such as altered sleep patterns or post-ECT confusion, may take months to resolve.

For patients with schizophrenia, remission is often a non-linear process with a risk of relapse if adequate care and monitoring are not maintained. As such, functional improvement during remission does not necessarily imply recovery or cure. Levels of support from family and employers often fluctuate depending on whether the patient is in an active episode or a remission phase. Targeted workplace adjustments, particularly in the initial months following an episode, can contribute significantly to stability and gradual reintegration into expected performance levels. Remission should not be equated with incompetence. At the same time, it must be acknowledged that aggressive treatments and recurrent episodes may have long-term psychological and cognitive effects. A more measured and supportive approach during both admission and remission, by clinicians and support systems alike, is therefore essential.

A further distinction is important. Even after returning to work or routine life, patients may ***continue to carry residual effects of both the episode and its treatment.*** *This may include incomplete understanding of the episodic experience, unanswered questions, and gaps in recollection,* *particularly where treatment has been aggressive or non-consensual. During remission, individuals may display what are termed negative symptoms, such as social withdrawal, difficulty with sustained communication, reduced emotional reciprocity, or diminished responsiveness. These behaviours should be understood as part of adjustment and recovery rather than disinterest or lack of effort.*

Support systems benefit from recognising this phase and responding with patience and caution. What may appear as limited engagement can function as a coping or recalibration mechanism. In early remission, maintenance dosages are often relatively high, which can contribute to sluggishness or reduced expressiveness. These effects are typically transient, and with time and appropriate support, a sense of normalcy and the smile can be restored.

With this context, the following section provides a non-exhaustive overview of mental health conditions across the spectrum, without ranking them by severity or urgency.

Major Psychotic Spectrum Conditions

1. Bipolar Disorder/Manic Depression

Bipolar disorder is characterised by extreme mood fluctuations, typically cycling between manic and depressive phases. Psychotic symptoms such as delusions or hallucinations may occur during severe or prolonged manic or depressive episodes, but they are not a defining feature of the disorder in all cases.

The depressive phase of bipolar disorder may include social withdrawal, low motivation, and reduced engagement. Clinically, these features are understood as mood-related and often improve as mood stabilises. In contrast, similar features in schizophrenia are described as negative symptoms and may persist beyond mood changes. From a patient's perspective, however, the lived experience of these states can overlap and may be difficult to distinguish.

Treatment commonly involves psychotherapy, mood stabilisers, and, where appropriate, antipsychotic medication. In cases where individuals exhibit persistent psychotic symptoms alongside prominent mood disturbances across episodes, a diagnosis of **schizoaffective disorder** may be considered.

Non-Psychotic but Overlapping Conditions

1. Depression

Depression is characterised by low mood, feelings of hopelessness, reduced motivation, and loss of interest in day-to-day activities. It may also be accompanied by suicidal thoughts, which can overlap with other conditions such as schizophrenia and bipolar disorder. When these symptoms arise, a holistic care plan is important and may include adjunct medication where clinically indicated.

Medication can help stabilise mood and reduce the intensity of symptoms, particularly during acute phases. However, medication alone does not alter underlying thought patterns, self-perception, or deeply held beliefs that contribute to low self-esteem. These aspects often require psychological intervention and time. Cognitive Behavioural Therapy, which focuses on identifying negative thought patterns and gradually reframing them, along with a balanced lifestyle that includes regular meals, hydration, physical activity, and supportive social connections, can play a significant role in coping with depression.

Depression may present episodically, but persistent depressive states that remain unchanged over extended periods require timely attention. The remission phase of schizophrenia can at times resemble an episodic depressive state, where mood is subdued and motivation remains low. With time and a holistic approach, emotional balance and functional stability can gradually return.

In no way, anywhere on the spectrum, does remission mean a permanent solution. It is an ongoing battle—one that can only be won by restructuring the self first, and then looking outward.

Restructuring in these situations may simply mean letting things be, and letting go of what no longer serves a purpose.

2. Anxiety

Anxiety is a state of constant worrying and overthinking, to the extent that it can lead to feelings of suffocation or panic attacks. One way of understanding anxiety is as an extension of the survival instinct. From primitive times, the human brain has been wired to cling to fear more readily than to optimism, and the capitalistic nature of society can further amplify this tendency.

Being content and not living beyond one's means can help mitigate material or performance-related anxiety. For emotional anxiety, such as feeling lost, unloved, or unreciprocated, there is often no quick external solution. Careful self-tending becomes important. Whether that self-tending happens internally through self-talk, through journaling, or with the support of a therapist is a personal choice. However, self-acceptance can significantly calm the mind, and the world outside may begin to feel more forgiving and tolerant. Yes, trust me.

3. Obsessive Compulsive Disorder (OCD)

OCD is a condition in which recurring thought patterns or behavioural patterns disturb the brain's rhythm or equilibrium. These thoughts or urges can arise suddenly, often in waves, and sometimes the most effective response is to allow the wave to pass.

Journaling common triggers or behaviours can help provide reassurance that a task has been completed. For instance, if you have OCD related to cleaning, make a note when cleaning is done. If you have OCD related to checking locks, make a simple note on your phone stating that the door is locked. If medication adherence is the concern, maintaining a medicine journal can help. Being systematic in this manner, along with Cognitive Behavioural Therapy, may be helpful in managing OCD.

4. Attention Deficit Hyperactivity Disorder (ADHD)

ADHD, as the name suggests, is characterised by difficulties with attention, and in some cases, hyperactivity. It commonly involves reduced focus, distractibility, fidgeting or frequent movement, and impulsivity. Impulsivity may sometimes appear as extended or rapid conversations on a topic, or as sudden knee-jerk responses.

ADHD is understood to involve differences in how the brain regulates attention, activity, and impulse control. In everyday life, this can feel like a mind that remains constantly in motion, even when there is no immediate stressor. Alongside Cognitive Behavioural Therapy, light physical activity such as walking or exercise, journaling, and structured routines can help channel excess mental energy.

Brief meditation practices, even for a few minutes, may help introduce pauses into habitual thought patterns. Journaling anxious or repetitive thoughts and returning to hobbies or interests that help provide focus can also be useful ways to direct attention more constructively.

5. Autism Spectrum Disorder (ASD)

Based on existing research, schizophrenia and autism spectrum disorder are recognised as distinct conditions. Research also suggests that individuals with ASD may have an increased likelihood of developing schizophrenia later in adulthood. ASD is typically diagnosed in childhood, whereas schizophrenia is more commonly diagnosed in adulthood. However, there can be overlap in certain features, particularly what are clinically described as negative or social functioning-related symptoms, such as social withdrawal, limited speech, and reduced emotional reciprocity.

ASD is also categorised into different levels based on support needs. Level 3 requires very substantial support in day-to-day functioning, Level 2 requires substantial support, and Level 1 requires some support.

Author's Note

In the author's lived experience, non-consensual and aggressive treatments, combined with lingering memory gaps, over-medication, and stigma, can alter social functioning and emotional responsiveness over time. The author reflects that these cumulative effects may resemble features often associated with Level 1 ASD, even when no such diagnosis previously existed. This is a personal reflection rather than a clinical assertion, but it highlights how long-term treatment impact and stigma can shape behaviour and self-perception.

CHAPTER FIFTEEN

WHO AND OTHER NOTEWORTHY STATISTICS

World Health Organization (WHO) states on its website that *"Schizophrenia causes psychosis, is associated with considerable disability and may affect all areas of life, including personal, family, social, educational, and occupational functioning. Stigma, discrimination, and violation of human rights of people with schizophrenia are common."*

The above excerpt from the WHO website highlights the significant emphasis placed on the rights of people living with schizophrenia. It also explicitly acknowledges the stigma, discrimination, and human rights violations that continue to be associated with the condition. Further, the WHO recognises schizophrenia as a major psychiatric disorder with wide-ranging personal and social impact.

Author's Note

From the author's personal experience, the first to withdraw during times of crisis is often the distant family. The immediate family, prima facie, bears the burden not necessarily by choice, but because of circumstance and the stigma attached to the ailment.

In the Indian context, the induction of spirals and the undue importance placed on Nominated Representatives create a different and concerning dynamic around patient consent and autonomy. **If any form**

of financial support, disability benefits, or unemployment assistance is to be provided, it should empower and accrue directly to the patient. Financial independence is often what gives patients the confidence and agency to make decisions for themselves, including the ability to walk away from unsafe or unhealthy situations when necessary.

Amidst this, the author found comfort in two important realities: first, that a few close friends stood by her through both humour and hardship; and second, that the diagnosis occurred close to the age of thirty-one, after formal education and initial work experience had already been completed. Despite the strain of ECT side effects and high maintenance dosages, the author managed to hold her ground for several years before choosing to speak openly. That decision, and the strength required for it, ultimately inspired this book.

What patients need is not the label of care-givers, but genuine empowerment: a place in society, financial independence, and the ability to express themselves and feel human. Most importantly, they need the power and resources to walk away when required, without their vulnerability becoming an avenue for others to assume undue decision-making authority.

According to the World Health Organization website, *"Schizophrenia affects approximately 23 million people worldwide, or about 1 in 345 people (0.29%). Among adults, the rate is estimated at 1 in 233 people (0.43%). It is not as common as many other mental disorders. Onset most often occurs during late adolescence and the twenties, and onset tends to occur earlier among men than among women."*

Published studies indicate that the risk of death by suicide is higher among individuals living with schizophrenia when compared with the general population. This underscores the importance of holistic care, and more critically, the need to empower affected individuals through meaningful subsidies and subsistence support. Social and occupational integration plays a vital role in long-term stability.

It is imperative that employers offer flexible work arrangements, and equally importantly, honour them in practice. Employers also need to understand the distinction between remission and cure. Remission does not imply full recovery, and patience, accommodation, and continuity of support are essential during this phase.

Are We Creating a System of Dissent in Mental Healthcare in India?

Whilst on this journey between remission and recovery in March 2026, I want to raise a very serious systemic issue.

Are there more dissenting patients like me out there in India? The procedural overlap between my two admissions in India, the non-consensual invasive procedures, transactional care settings, and the humiliation of being dragged barefoot with no awareness of legal recourse raise a serious concern: the power we are attributing to mental health establishments, which remain civilian institutions in nature. With a well-intended but loosely implemented MHCA 2017 (Mental Healthcare Act, 2017), are we creating a system of dissent among patients?

Are we jeopardising adult rights by giving Nominated Representatives undue decision-making authority and invoking emergencies prior to examination, thereby setting the spiral in motion? Are we diminishing the autonomy of adult mental health patients in India and forcing them to become dependent on caregivers or presumed NRs for decision-making?

In the author's opinion, we are.

And then we ask a more systemic question: what is the patient's insight into the ailment before going to work, before drafting a legal document, before living a normal day-to-day life, and perhaps even before breathing?

The same insight that invasive procedures may erase in the name of treatment due to permanent memory loss, while the memories of coercive admission—and more importantly, the delusions—remain intact.

Are mental health establishments above the law in this country simply because they belong to a profession traditionally considered noble? Is the profession still noble when heavy private equity investments are entering private healthcare? Is it?

Why are we then asking questions about increasing suicide rates among mental health patients, especially the youth, in India?

Is the system failing them?

Are we, through loosely implemented safeguards and unchecked emergency powers, creating a system where patients lose trust in the very institutions meant to protect them?

Nine years and counting.

CHAPTER SIXTEEN

MHCA, 2017 (The Mental Health Care Act, 2017)

The Mental Healthcare Act, 2017 was enacted following India's ratification of the United Nations Convention on the Rights of Persons with Disabilities in 2007. The Act was intended to shift mental healthcare toward a rights-based framework.

Mental Health Review Boards (MHRBs) are central to the implementation of the Mental Healthcare Act, 2017. However, they are required to function at both the state and district levels, and in practice their presence appears limited.

Nearly nine years after the enactment of the Act, this gap suggests that budgetary constraints and the prioritisation of communicable diseases and physical health conditions may continue to take precedence over mental health in India.

Mental Health Review Boards (MHRBs): Status of Patient Access (March 2026)

The Mental Healthcare Act, 2017 provides for Mental Health Review Boards (MHRBs) at the state and district levels to safeguard patient rights, review supported admissions, and hear grievances. These Boards are also intended to oversee Advance Directives and requests related to Nominated Representatives. They are intended to be quasi-judicial bodies in nature.

Several states have formally notified MHRBs on paper. However, publicly accessible mechanisms through which patients can approach these Boards remain extremely difficult to identify in practice. Most state notifications provide only lists of board members without clear procedures for filing complaints, submitting Advance Directives, or requesting review.

Karnataka's e-Manas platform is one of the few attempts to create an online interface for such services. However, the patient portal intended for filing Advance Directives and grievances does not appear to be functional at present.

Nearly nine years after the enactment of the Mental Healthcare Act, 2017, accessible and patient-facing systems for approaching MHRBs remain limited, leaving many patients without a clear pathway to exercise their legal rights.

The Act was enacted in the right spirit, with the intent of making mental healthcare more accessible and non-discriminatory. It is designed to be patient-centric and broadly aligned with mental healthcare frameworks in developed countries, where patients are expected to participate in decisions regarding their course of treatment within the confines of the law, and where clear redressal mechanisms exist to address any overrides of consent. The Act also serves as a counterbalance and checkpoint for mental health practitioners, particularly because mental health diagnoses are largely observational and are not typically supported by definitive diagnostic tests.

However, in practice, a framework that was crafted to protect patient rights may sometimes appear to function in the opposite manner. Patchy implementation, combined with a mindset that often prioritises family members as Nominated Representatives without adequate scrutiny, can make it easier to override patient consent. As a result, despite its progressive intent, the Act remains far from fully protecting patients in the Indian context.

The roles of the Nominated Representative and Advance Directives have already been discussed in earlier sections. However, if there is one provision that warrants reiteration, it is the misapplication or misinterpretation of the emergency provision, which brings prevailing practices into sharp focus. The author has also discussed Section 27, which relates to the right to legal aid, as well as Sections 4 and 89, which address capacity and supported admission.

Emergency Provision (Section 94)

Section 94: "*(1) Notwithstanding anything contained in this Act, any medical treatment, including treatment for mental illness, may be provided by any registered medical practitioner to a person with mental illness either at a health establishment or in the community, subject to the informed consent of the nominated representative, where the nominated representative is available, and where it is immediately necessary to prevent— (a) death or irreversible harm to the health of the person; or (b) the person inflicting serious harm to himself or to others; or (c) the person causing serious damage to property belonging to himself or to others where such behaviour is believed to flow directly from the person's mental illness.*

Explanation.—For the purposes of this section, "emergency treatment" includes transportation of the person with mental illness to a nearest mental health establishment for assessment. (2) Nothing in this section shall allow any medical officer or psychiatrist to give to the person with mental illness medical treatment which is not directly related to the emergency treatment specified under sub-section (1). (3) Nothing in this section shall allow any medical officer or psychiatrist to use electro-convulsive therapy as a form of treatment. (4) The emergency treatment referred to in this section shall be limited to seventy-two hours or till the person with mental illness has been assessed at a mental health establishment, whichever is earlier: Provided that during a disaster or emergency declared by the appropriate Government, the period of emergency treatment referred to in this sub-section may extend up to seven days."

Author's Note

Section 94 is widely and loosely interpreted in private practice. In my experience, the process typically begins with invoking "emergency" and assuming lack of capacity. The injectable used to sedate me was not a light sleep aid; it initiated a memory spiral. I do not know the exact composition, but its effect on my nervous system was profound — my subsequent treatment became a blur. After both admissions in India, I experienced permanent memory loss for the in-patient stay and a few days after discharge. I remember no meaningful psychotherapy, no treating team, and no clear recall of discharge; I only learned my diagnosis from the discharge summary.

The memory spiral began with emergency sedation and was then exacerbated by repeated ECT and overlapping high-dose medications and long-acting injectables. In practice, PANSS (Positive and Negative Syndrome Scale) scores may initially worsen and later show a marginal decline signalling slight improvement following this cascade — a change that, in my view, may partly reflect treatment-induced cognitive blunting and reduced patient participation rather than meaningful therapeutic recovery.

In one episode I was in my hotel room when staff entered. A woman first spoke with me; then two others sat on me so I could not breathe. I was injected in my pelvic area, dragged barefoot to an ambulance, sedated, and upon arrival at the hospital woken up from sedation and dragged barefoot inside the premise. I saw my mother standing at a distance with a resolute look as if coercion was justified; that is my last clear memory before a month-long blur. There was no psychiatric pre-examination. For the first episode I had been at work the day before admission; although confused and delusional, I could understand basic English and could have participated in decisions had my capacity not been undermined by the emergency sequence.

Because capacity was presumed lost in the emergency, decisions became a dialogue between doctors and the Nominated Representative, with no meaningful participation from me, despite the patient-centred intent of the Mental Healthcare Act, 2017. CBT and psychotherapy were billed and recorded, yet I have no lived memory of attending them; the sessions did not build insight or continuity because the patient could not retain context and had permanent memory loss for the entire periods of hospitalisation and a few days after discharge.

The cumulative aftermath has been profound: extended low motivation, extreme photosensitivity, difficulty writing, and cognitive side-effects that persisted for over a year. These are not trivial inconveniences but realities that reshape daily life and the ability to engage in recovery.

I raise this not as an abstract complaint but as a call to those responsible for implementing the law: the emergency provisions, as applied, can become a shortcut around capacity safeguards. Without stricter controls and accountability, emergency invocation can systematically erase a patient's narrative and agency. I cannot be the only one; this requires oversight and reform.

Right to Legal Aid (Section 27)

Section 27: "*(1) A person with mental illness shall be entitled to receive free legal services to exercise any of his rights given under this Act. (2) It shall be the duty of magistrate, police officer, person in charge of such custodial institution as may be prescribed or medical officer or mental health professional in charge of a mental health 17 establishment to inform the person with mental illness that he is entitled to free legal services under the Legal Services Authorities Act, 1987 (39 of 1987) or other relevant laws or under any order of the court if so ordered and provide the contact details of the availability of services.*"

Author's Note

A right that cannot be remembered, exercised, or explained at the point of care remains a right only on paper.

This implies that it is the institution's prerogative to make patients aware of their rights and their access to legal aid. However, during my two admissions in India, I barely remember being conscious or able to participate meaningfully. To the best of my recollection, this right was neither explained during admission nor discussed later during remission. During the brief and highly transactional consultations I recall with my psychiatrist during remission and recovery, I do not remember Real conversations that happen only in a café" any discussion about patient legal rights, the importance of an Advance Directive, or the appointment of a Nominated Representative to protect my interests. My psychiatrist was also aware that my relationship with my family was strained.

In India, legal aid does not appear to be directly integrated with hospital admission procedures, and patients are not typically provided with a list of lawyers upon arrival to help navigate the process. Mental health patients are entitled to free legal aid from state and district legal services authorities. However, based on web searches, the author was unable to find any readily available lists specifically for the appointment of lawyers for mental health–related redressal under national, state, or district authorities.

During my treatment abroad, I recall being provided with a list of advocates or lawyers, and I also met a few of them during my stay in the ward. I had access to my rights, I remembered the events clearly, and I exercised those rights even while experiencing delusional symptoms.

Capacity (Section 4 and Section 89)

Section 4: "*Capacity to make mental healthcare and treatment decisions.—(1) Every person, including a*

person with mental illness shall be deemed to have capacity to make decisions regarding his mental

healthcare or treatment if such person has ability to—

(a) understand the information that is relevant to take a decision on the treatment or admission or personal assistance; or

(b) appreciate any reasonably foreseeable consequence of a decision or lack of decision on the treatment or admission or personal assistance; or

(c) communicate the decision under sub-clause (a) by means of speech, expression, gesture or any other means.

(2) The information referred to in sub-section (1) shall be given to a person using simple language, which such person understands or in sign language or visual aids or any other means to enable him to understand the information.

(3) Where a person makes a decision regarding his mental healthcare or treatment which is perceived by others as inappropriate or wrong, that by itself, shall not mean that the person does not have the capacity to make mental healthcare or treatment decision, so long as the person has the capacity to make mental healthcare or treatment decision under sub-section (1)."

Section 89 (excerpt): "*Admission and treatment of persons with mental illness, with high support needs, in mental health establishment, up to thirty days (supported admission).*

(6) Every person with mental illness admitted under this section shall be provided treatment after taking into account,—

(a) an advance directive if any; or
(b) informed consent of the patient with the support of his nominated representative subject to the provisions of sub-section (7).

(7) If a person with the mental illness admitted under this section requires nearly hundred per cent. support from his nominated representative in making a decision in respect of his treatment, the nominated representative may temporarily consent to the treatment plan of such person on his behalf.

(8) In case where consent has been given under sub-section (7), the medical officer or mental health professional in charge of the mental health establishment shall record such consent in the medical records and review the capacity of the patient to give consent every seven days.

(9) The medical officer or mental health professional in charge of the mental health establishment shall report the concerned Board,—

(a) within three days the admissions of a woman or a minor;
(b) within seven days the admission of any person not being a woman or minor."

Author's Note

Capacity is presumed to exist until proved otherwise. During one of my episodes, I was going to the office one day before my hospitalisation. I was confused and distracted, but my comprehension and memory during both episodes were intact, even though I was symptomatic and delusional.

When the spiral began, I started to lose ground, and that could have been used as a double-edged sword. First, to show incapacity and exclude the patient from decision-making by pointing to declining or marginally improving PANSS scores during the induced spiral. Second, to justify further aggressive procedures that continue the spiral and meet transactional targets. In such a situation, the outcome appears favourable for the treating team but deeply detrimental for the patient.

When consent is taken away, MHRBs are required to be informed and a reassessment of capacity must be performed every seven days under the Mental Healthcare Act, 2017. I have no recollection of any such assessments, and MHRBs themselves remain limited or absent in many places even several years after the enactment of the Act.

I often observe even seasoned professionals overlapping the concepts of capacity and clinical insight into the ailment. Capacity, as presumed under the Act, is based on the ability to understand relevant information, which in the author's understanding includes language, diagnosis, treatment options, and the consequences of a chosen course of action. The course of treatment need not necessarily be the one recommended by the medical team, but the one that the patient consents to within the framework of the law. Refusal to comply should not automatically amount to incapacity.

Clinical insight, on the other hand, refers to awareness or understanding of the underlying ailment, which can be highly subjective in mental health from an experiential, exposure, and therapeutic perspective, including insight developed through CBT.

The author has experienced three psychotic episodes, two of which could be classified as acute. In the author's opinion, during both admissions in India she did not lack capacity or basic language processing until the point at which the induced spiral began.

More concerning, in the author's lived experience during the two admissions in India, the memory of the delusions remained intact, but due to invasive and aggressive procedures the therapy and CBT sessions did not integrate. The author did not remember the names of the treatment team or what they looked like. She walked out of the hospitals with permanent memory gaps and psychological discontinuity.

Moreover, years after undergoing these treatments, the author is now facing resistance when attempting to file an Advance Directive, with psychiatrists recommending personality assessments to evaluate the same insight that the author believes was undermined by the earlier aggressive interventions, leaving behind only memories of delusional experiences. Please refer to Chapter 13 for context on the Advance Directive draft and the challenges currently faced by the author.

The author also wishes to contrast this with her treatment abroad. During an acute psychotic phase, her capacity was not immediately questioned. She was given time to stabilise and was not overridden. Invasive procedures were suggested but not imposed. One-on-one sessions with psychologists may have helped her process the delusions more constructively rather than relying primarily on increased medication dosages. However, that request was not fulfilled.

At the end of this section, the author wishes to reiterate that nothing in this country should stand above the law. Emergency provisions must operate within clear legal and ethical boundaries.

Medical staff should not enter a person's private premises without appropriate legal presence or safeguards. Sedation prior to examination in an emergency should not become a default response. Physical coercion should never be treated as routine. **Paramedics and nursing staff, who are often the first point of contact in emergencies, require continued training in mental health awareness, de-escalation, and patient dignity.** Association with a medical establishment should not translate into an assumption that force is acceptable when dealing with a dissenting or distressed patient.

The author's experiences, both in India and abroad, have left lasting impressions about how emergencies involving mental health patients are sometimes handled. In one instance abroad, the emergency holding area was small, dimly lit, and restrictive. Drinking water was scarce and the sanitation conditions were poor. While delusional and disoriented, the author recalls being physically handled by police, and dragged into an emergency room by paramedics/security guards after refusing to enter voluntarily. Some of the staff involved appeared to be of Indian origin and were conversing casually on the sidelines in Hindi, making evening plans while the situation unfolded — a memory that remains deeply distressing.

In another moment during the same admission, nurses attempted to draw blood while the author was still delusional and agitated. Guards restrained her arms holding them upright while pressure was applied to the torso so that the procedure could be completed quickly. The resulting bruise on the left arm was significant and was not attended to during the emergency stay. The author recalls the broader hospital environment continuing its routine operations while this situation unfolded, leaving a lasting impression of how little attention was given to the patient's distress.

These memories illustrate a larger concern. When a patient is delusional or lacks insight, it is often assumed that their testimony will not carry weight or that their recollection of events will be dismissed. This assumption risks normalising coercive behaviour and undermining the dignity of mental health patients.

Emergency care must prioritise safety, but safety should not come at the cost of empathy, restraint, and respect for basic rights. Without stronger training, oversight, and accountability mechanisms, emergency provisions can easily drift away from their intended purpose and become instruments of convenience rather than care.

Emergency provisions exist to protect life, not to erase dignity.

CHAPTER SEVENTEEN

MENTAL HEALTH AND UNION BUDGET 2026-27

The Union Budget 2026–27 placed increased emphasis on mental health as part of overall public health strengthening. Announcements included higher allocations for healthcare infrastructure, the phased establishment of NIMHANS-2 in North India, the upgradation of select existing mental health institutions, and the expansion of training capacity for doctors and support staff. The budget also focused on improving emergency and trauma care services. In addition, Tele-MANAS received further policy support, strengthening its role as a nationwide tele-consultation and mental health helpline. However, there is no standalone budget allocation specifically for mental health.

Based on research from credible sources, there was no mention of patient rights, updates on the implementation of the Mental Healthcare Act, 2017, or the establishment of Mental Health Review Boards (MHRBs) in the Union Budget 2026–27. This is notable given that, nearly nine years after the enactment of the Act, MHRBs appear to remain limited or non-operational in many places.

As a patient, the focus on expanding mental health infrastructure raised more questions than answers in a system that is already short of psychiatrists, psychologists, and other support staff, in addition to broader infrastructure constraints. It raises a basic question: if monitoring of patient rights through MHRBs and stricter implementation of the MHCA

2017 are not even mentioned, does this push practical ground-level solutions further away? Instead of strengthening and better managing the current infrastructure and ensuring the establishment of MHRBs, funding directed primarily toward building new infrastructure without corresponding accountability or redressal mechanisms may risk widening existing gaps.

In an economy where government subsistence support for mental health patients remains limited, and where many schemes do not explicitly recognise schizophrenia as a disability category, it becomes important that private mental healthcare is appropriately monitored. Private care is often expensive, and many patients experience consultations as highly transactional. To ease the burden on public infrastructure, stronger regulatory oversight of private mental healthcare in India may therefore be necessary. Residential treatment programs can be costly, as can follow-up consultations during remission.

It is important to understand the gravity of the situation and the role that a regulated and more accessible private mental healthcare system could play in making care available to people from different sections of society. Regulation of private healthcare may also help reduce waiting times in public healthcare systems.

Moreover, whether one has experienced a physical health challenge or not, nearly everyone passes through phases of mental stress at different stages of life — childhood, adolescence, adulthood, or old age. Mental healthcare therefore requires a more structured and carefully planned framework within the broader health system, in the author's opinion.

Author's Note

Based on conversations with psychiatrists in September 2025, the author enquired whether schizophrenia was classified as a disability and whether it was eligible for a government-issued disability certificate. The psychiatrist mentioned that it is a treatable condition. However, based on further research, the author confirms that schizophrenia does qualify for a disability certificate, subject to certain conditions, such as having at least a two-year history of the illness and undergoing an IDEAS assessment.

Please refer to Chapter 18 for further details.

Further, the government is investing in and promoting Tele-MANAS, which is an excellent initiative. However, as discussed in Chapter 13, the same was used as a justification to deny the author a certificate of fitness to draft her Advance Directive in her personal space, thereby impairing her right to sign and draft her own treatment plan at a time when only a maintenance dose was being administered and no hospitalisation had taken place.

This appears rather strange and counterintuitive. It raises a basic question: is the Indian private mental healthcare system meeting the government halfway? Are they truly aligned in their approach and implementation strategies?

CHAPTER EIGHTEEN

The Rights of Persons with Disabilities Act (RPwD), 2016

India ratified the UN Convention on the Rights of Persons with Disabilities (UNCRPD) in 2007, which prompted the replacement of the earlier 1995 law with a new rights-based statute. The Rights of Persons with Disabilities Act, 2016 was passed in December 2016 (with rules issued in mid-2017) to align Indian law with the UN treaty framework.

The Act significantly broadened the scope of disability. Official categories expanded from 7 to 21 and are now defined in social and functional terms rather than purely medical ones. The law also enshrines enforceable rights—such as reservation quotas, accessibility provisions, and legal protections—backed by special courts and penalties, moving away from the largely advisory approach of the 1995 law.

The Act also specifically defines mental illness, in alignment with the provisions of the Mental Healthcare Act, 2017.

However, implementation still remains patchy due to insufficient oversight and enforcement mechanisms. There are not enough State Commissioners for Persons with Disabilities to monitor implementation, review safeguards, and address complaints. There is also a scarcity of special courts at the state level.

To apply for a disability certificate for mental disability under the Act, a patient must undergo psychological assessment. One commonly used evaluation tool is the IDEAS assessment (Indian Disability Evaluation and Assessment Scale), which rates mental disability across four parameters: self-care, interpersonal activities, communication and understanding, and work.

However, based on available research, the process of obtaining a disability certificate can often be tedious and time-consuming. This is primarily due to administrative procedures and the requirement for detailed medical documentation.

Disability Criterion in Developed Nations vs India

Based on research from credible sources, it is observed that developed nations such as the United States and the United Kingdom have a more identifiable and less rigid framework for determining and classifying disability. These countries typically consider factors that affect the day-to-day life of an individual, including self-care, mobility, basic living activities, and the ability to work. The criteria are generally clearer and aim at either reintegration into society, financial support, or both.

In contrast, India's system relies largely on percent-based disability ratings. By law, a person must have at least 40% disability (as assessed through tools such as the IDEAS scale) to qualify for most benefits. The government has also proposed color-coded UDID (Unique Disability Identification) cards: white for less than 40%, yellow for 40–80%, and blue for more than 80% disability. Critics argue that such categorisation can appear arbitrary. For instance, current rules assign a flat 40% disability rating to certain specific learning disabilities (such as dyslexia), even though the severity of functional limitation may vary widely between individuals. Some experts argue that this approach does not always reflect real-world needs, such as the ability to perform daily tasks or maintain work-related activities based on current health status and medical evidence. Sharp cut-offs may therefore exclude individuals who experience significant impairment but fall just below the 40% threshold.

Another contrast arises in the treatment of mental illness. India's guidelines require a mental health condition (such as schizophrenia) to be chronic—typically lasting two years or more—before a permanent disability certificate may be granted. In countries such as the United States or the United Kingdom, disability determination generally focuses on current functional limitation rather than the duration of the illness. Some experts suggest that the two-year requirement in India may delay access to support and may unintentionally reinforce stigma by implying that only long-term cases qualify for assistance.

Schizophrenia and Disability Support in India

Schizophrenia is explicitly included under "mental illness" in the law, but in practice it receives limited focused attention. Commentators note that the Act, in effect, primarily addresses four major mental illnesses—schizophrenia, bipolar disorder, obsessive–compulsive disorder (OCD), and dementia—while many other conditions receive comparatively little emphasis.

Even within this framework, several analyses suggest that mental illnesses remain underemphasised in India's disability support system. There appears to be no government welfare scheme dedicated solely to schizophrenia; patients must rely on the same general disability programmes (such as pensions, health schemes, and social support benefits) that are available to all persons with disabilities.

This gasp may partly reflect the continuing stigma and systemic oversight surrounding mental health conditions.

Notable Government Schemes for Persons with Disabilities

India does offer several social-support programmes for certified persons with disabilities (PwDs). For example:

1. Disability Pension

Low-income PwDs (People with Disabilities) can receive a monthly stipend under social security schemes. In many states this ranges between ₹500 and ₹1,200 per month depending on the assessed level of disability. One source notes that ₹500 is provided for 40–75% disability and ₹1,200 for disability of 75% or more.

2. Tax Deductions

Section 80U of the Income Tax Act provides tax deductions to persons with disabilities — ₹75,000 per year if disability is 40% or more and ₹ 1,25,000 if disability is 80% or more. Caregivers can also claim similar benefits under Section 80DD.

3. Travel Concessions

Certified persons with disabilities are eligible for subsidised transport benefits, including concessional bus passes and rail fare discounts.

4. Health Insurance

Schemes such as Swavlamban health insurance provide coverage up to ₹2 lakh annually. National programmes such as Ayushman Bharat now include mental healthcare in their benefit packages.

These examples demonstrate that certain forms of support exist, including pensions, tax benefits, travel concessions, and insurance coverage. However, the pension amounts remain relatively modest. For many persons with disabilities, it is important that subsistence support covers basic living expenses such as rent and utilities.

In my observation abroad, persons with disabilities often receive structured subsistence support that helps cover essential living costs. In the case of conditions such as schizophrenia, each episode can add substantial cognitive and functional strain, with recovery sometimes taking months or even years.

Beyond the emotional impact of the episodes themselves, aggressive treatments and prolonged recovery periods can affect the patient's long-term socio-economic stability and social reintegration. In this context, there is a strong case for the government to consider providing more meaningful subsistence support for persons with disabilities, including those living with mental illness.

Ideally, such benefits should accrue directly to the patient rather than being routed primarily through Nominated Representatives or caregivers. Encouraging adult rights and independent living among persons with mental illness can play an important role in long-term rehabilitation.

Finally, the process for obtaining disability certificates may benefit from further streamlining, particularly in light of the administrative and procedural challenges discussed earlier.

While the Rights of Persons with Disabilities Act, 2016 represents an important step toward a rights-based framework, its practical impact ultimately depends on how effectively disability recognition translates into meaningful social support. For persons living with conditions such as schizophrenia, recovery often involves long periods of cognitive adjustment, social reintegration, and economic uncertainty. In such circumstances, disability recognition should not merely be a procedural classification but a mechanism that enables dignity, subsistence security, and independent living. Strengthening disability certification processes, expanding subsistence support, and ensuring that benefits reach the patient directly could play a significant role in bridging the gap between legislative intent and lived reality.

When I Met a Person with a Disability in a Foreign Ward Setting

I am not denying that even internationally there is scope for better implementation of mental health rights and practices, especially around emergency curtailment scenarios.

However, I strongly feel that rights are still protected, and overriding them may not be as brazen as in India.

During my final weeks in the ward abroad, I was assisted during my time-outs by a nurse or hospital staff member who had autism spectrum disorder. He used to wear a badge indicating this. We never discussed it during our interactions, but he was simply kind and normal to speak with. He would make me coffee and encourage me to participate in art activities, which I often found too trivial for an accountant who is more comfortable with mathematics.

Interacting with him and seeing him integrate into society while living with a disability was very uplifting for someone like me.

I have also seen at least one instance of a person with cerebral palsy working at a bus ticket counter in Canada.

This brings into question a very strange dynamic in India, where Nominated Representatives (NRs) are presumed to be the primary caretakers and the idea of independent living is rarely given prominence. This is particularly concerning given that many patients with schizophrenia either already have strained relationships with their families or develop strained relationships after families are given the authority to override patient consent and take independent treatment decisions. In India, it sometimes appears as though there is an NR–doctor nexus.

Based on research, there remains a large segment of government officials, medical practitioners, and lawmakers who appear to operate within the traditional Hindu Undivided Family (HUF) mindset, where family authority is treated as supreme. In contrast, the younger generation—especially those navigating mental health challenges—often prefers independent decision-making and independent living.

It's my body: I decide.

CHAPTER NINETEEN

Digital Personal Data Protection Act, 2023 (DPDP)

The Digital Personal Data Protection Act, 2023 (DPDP Act) is India's statutory framework for processing digital personal data. It was enacted to balance individual control over personal data with legitimate uses of data for services, governance and commerce; the Act received Presidential assent on 11 August 2023.

Key Provisions

1. Data principal rights

Individuals (data principals) gain defined rights such as access, correction and erasure of their digital personal data, and the ability to withdraw consent where processing depends on it.

2. Obligations of fiduciaries

Organisations that hold/process personal data (data fiduciaries) must follow purpose limitation, data-minimisation, reasonable security measures, and obligations such as breach notification and record-keeping.

3. Consent and lawful bases

The Act centres consent for most processing, with specified lawful exceptions and safeguards for legitimate uses.

4. Adjudication and penalties

A Data Protection Board (adjudicatory body) can investigate breaches, issue corrective orders (including erasure), and levy penalties for non-compliance; the Act empowers significant remedies to enforce standards.

Practical Implications for People with Mental-Health Conditions

1. Stronger Claim to Their Records

The Act reinforces a patient's standing as the data principal: mental-health patients can formally request access, correction or deletion of digital records held by hospitals, tele-medicine platforms, labs or apps. This creates a legal channel distinct from clinical statutes to seek one's information.

2. Consent Complexity in Crisis

Because consent is a central legal basis, situations where a patient lacked capacity (acute psychosis, sedation, emergency admissions) raise difficult questions about whether consent given then was valid and which processing is permissible now. Practically, healthcare providers must document lawful bases and any emergency exceptions carefully.

For individuals who have experienced emergency or assisted psychiatric admissions, the application of data rights raises a more nuanced question. Mental health law generally recognizes that decision-making capacity may be temporarily impaired during an acute episode, which can justify short-term reliance on nominated representatives or emergency safeguards. However, such determinations are inherently time-specific. Once the individual is no longer hospitalized and is able to make informed decisions, the presumption of capacity ordinarily returns. In that context, continued reliance on past emergency admission frameworks to restrict access to personal medical records—or to require nominated representative consent for the release of those records at a later stage—can become questionable when the request is made by the patient in a stable, non-hospitalized state. The patient remains the primary subject of the information recorded during treatment, and the ability to access those records may be essential for understanding the trajectory of care, assessing the basis of past decisions, and reclaiming one's own narrative of illness and recovery, particularly in situations involving permanent memory loss.

3. Security and Vendor Risk

Hospitals and digital health vendors must now treat psychiatric records as high-risk: the DPDP expectations for breach reporting, DPIAs (Data Protection Impact Assessment) and vendor oversight mean tighter controls — but also greater operational demands on health providers. Breach or misuse of psychiatric data can carry serious privacy harms for patients.

4. Complaints Route

If a mental-health patient's access or data rights are denied, the Data Protection Board provides a statutory remediation path (independent of clinical review boards), which can order remedial measures or penalties.

Critique & Drawbacks

1. Operational Burden on Health Providers

The DPDP regime imposes compliance (DPIAs, DPOs, audits) that many hospitals — especially smaller or public ones — will struggle to implement quickly; gaps in capacity risk uneven protection and may slow access to care.

2. Consent vs Emergency Care Tension

The Act's consent focus can clash with clinical realities: emergencies and impaired capacity are not neatly handled by a consent-centric law, so patient care decisions must be carefully documented to avoid later disputes. This creates legal-clinical friction in psychiatric crises.

3. Implementation Lag and Enforcement Uncertainty

While the Board has strong powers on paper, practical enforcement, rule-making and sectoral guidance (healthcare-specific protocols) will take time; until then, frontline clinicians and hospitals may rely on cautious, variable policies (some of which may restrict access).

4. Costs and Inequality

Compliance costs (technology, audits, legal advice) may push smaller providers to defensive practices (over-redaction, blanket denials) or pass costs to patients; this risks unequal privacy protections across the system.

Author's Note

In February 2026, I formally reached out to the hospital where I had been treated to request access to my personal medical records. After waiting for nearly a month and sending a reminder, I received a response declining to release the records and making access contingent on written consent from the presumed NR, citing assisted admission and internal safety protocols. At the time of making this request, I was in a stable state and capable of making independent decisions. My request was grounded in my rights as an adult patient under the Mental Healthcare Act, 2017, as well as broader constitutional protections relating to autonomy, privacy, and informational self-determination. It was also consistent with emerging data rights under the Digital Personal Data Protection Act, 2023, and the broader transparency principles reflected in the Right to Information framework. The refusal therefore raises important questions regarding patient capacity, ownership of personal medical information, and the right to access one's own treatment history.

Beyond the legal questions lies a more personal one. As a mental-health patient who experienced **permanent memory loss** for the duration of my hospital stay, I have no recollection of the conversations, therapy sessions, or discussions that reportedly informed an aggressive course of treatment. I continue to remember the delusional experiences from that period, but not the therapy that was provided at significant cost. I believe I have the right to know what I said, what questions were asked, and what narrative about my condition shaped those clinical decisions. I also wish to understand whether statements made by my nominated representatives—family members with whom I do not co-inhabit—may have unintentionally exaggerated or misrepresented situations out of frustration or confusion. Access to these records is therefore not merely administrative; it is a matter of reclaiming my own words, understanding the trajectory of treatment, and finding closure after a period that had profound consequences for my body and life.

I left the hospital with no memory of signing my discharge documents, including a behavioural agreement that restricted my ability to leave the house without my parents' permission. The hospital later cited this agreement in correspondence as part of the therapeutic process, despite the fact that I have no recollection of signing it. In effect, an adult signature appears to have been obtained during a period of complete memory loss, and that document is now being relied upon as evidence of consent. These questions remain unresolved. As of March 2026, the situation continues to unfold.

While the hospital has cited assisted admission and safety protocols to justify withholding my records, it is important to recognize that capacity under the Mental Healthcare Act is both time-specific and decision-specific. A temporary impairment during an emergency admission cannot automatically negate the presumption of capacity once the patient has stabilized. My request for records was made in a non-hospitalized and stable state, where the law presumes that an adult patient possesses decision-making capacity. In this context, continuing to treat the request as dependent on Nominated Representative consent raises legitimate questions about the patient's autonomy and ownership of their own medical information, particularly in situations of permanent memory loss, where the patient no longer remembers her own narrative, her own words, or the conversations that informed an aggressive course of treatment.

The DPDP Act is a clear advance: it gives people legal standing over their digital data and creates an enforcement route outside clinical regulation. For psychiatric patients the law promises real gains — clearer access, formal remedies, and stronger incentives for secure handling — but only if implementation is sensitive to clinical realities (capacity, emergencies) and if regulators produce health-specific guidance rapidly. Otherwise, the well-intentioned rules risk adding procedural friction to already fraught moments of care.

CHAPTER TWENTY

Governance, Financialization, and Patient Exposure in India's Private Hospitals

Private hospitals in India have shifted rapidly from physician-led institutions to investor-backed corporate entities. That structural change has important consequences for board composition, the balance between profit and care, and frontline exposure of non-physician staff. This chapter documents governance patterns, regulatory gaps for allied health workers, and emerging private equity (PE) dynamics, and compares India's experience with recent evidence from the United States, Canada, and the UK.

Board Structure and Who Actually Governs Hospitals in India

Large private hospitals and hospital chains increasingly operate as corporate firms with boards dominated by business, legal and finance professionals rather than practicing clinicians. Promoter families, corporate executives, independent directors and investor representatives commonly occupy board seats; clinical representation is often limited to a small number of senior (sometimes retired) doctors or advisory roles rather than operational leadership on the governing board. This corporate governance model mirrors broader trends across Indian corporate firms and is well documented in sector studies.

This composition has implications: financial performance metrics, investor returns and operational efficiency targets are frequently prioritized at board level — sometimes at the expense of clinical priorities such as conservative staffing levels, emergency preparedness, or non-revenue clinical services. Case studies of regulatory gaps and "decentred" regulation highlight how governance incentives shape operational choices in practice.

Clinical Representation: Token or Substantive?

Where boards include clinicians, representation often takes the form of non-executive or retired doctors and medical advisors — useful for prestige and advice, but not always empowered to counterbalance investor objectives in executive committees (finance, remuneration, M&A). Multiple reviews warn that genuine clinical governance (clinical quality, safety committees, empowered chief medical officers with board access) is frequently weaker in investor-led models. Strengthening the minimum clinical presence on boards (e.g., named clinical directors, mandatory medical quality committees) is a clear governance remedy suggested in the literature.

Why Healthcare Cannot Be Treated Like Other Hospitality Sectors

Private hospitals are sometimes compared with other service industries such as hotels, tourism, or hospitality because they involve infrastructure management, service delivery, and private investment. However, healthcare differs fundamentally from these sectors due to structural characteristics that limit the effectiveness of ordinary market competition.

Healthcare markets are characterized by significant information asymmetry between patients and providers. Patients generally lack the medical expertise required to evaluate the necessity or appropriateness of treatments and must therefore rely on the judgment of physicians and healthcare institutions. Because patients cannot independently assess medical decisions in the same way they might evaluate other services, healthcare markets function differently from typical consumer markets and require stronger regulatory oversight. Research comparing public and private healthcare systems in developing countries highlights that patients often cannot evaluate the quality or necessity of care before treatment, reinforcing the need for stronger governance and regulatory frameworks.

Second, healthcare is often delivered under conditions of urgency or medical necessity, which significantly limits patient choice and the ability to compare prices or providers. Unlike hospitality services, where consumers can evaluate alternatives in advance, medical treatment frequently occurs during emergencies when immediate care is required. A major systematic review comparing public and private healthcare systems across developing countries found that patients often cannot evaluate or delay care decisions, making healthcare markets structurally different from ordinary service industries and requiring stronger regulatory oversight.

Third, healthcare institutions operate under professional and ethical obligations that extend beyond commercial service provision. Hospitals must maintain clinical governance systems, infection control standards, and safety protocols because clinical errors can result in severe injury or death. The global patient safety framework published by the World Health Organization emphasizes that healthcare systems require strong regulatory oversight precisely because patient vulnerability and treatment complexity create risks not present in typical service industries.

For these reasons, health policy scholars generally conclude that healthcare markets require stronger regulation of ownership, governance, and pricing structures than other service sectors. Comparative analyses of public and private healthcare systems consistently emphasize that patient vulnerability and information asymmetry justify more robust regulatory frameworks.

Workforce Regulation and Patient Exposure: The Paramedic and Nursing Gap

Healthcare differs fundamentally from other service sectors because patients often enter the system under conditions of urgency and with limited ability to evaluate medical decisions independently. Emergency departments typically rely on **triage systems**, where patients are assessed immediately on arrival in order to determine the urgency and nature of treatment required. This initial triage point is often the first stage at which clinical decision-making begins, and it shapes the pathway for subsequent medical evaluation and treatment. Research on emergency department processes shows that triage is usually the **first point of contact in emergency care**, where patients are assessed and prioritized before seeing physicians, making early observations and documentation crucial to later clinical decisions.

In many emergency situations, **nurses, paramedics, or emergency medical responders encounter the patient first**, particularly in pre-hospital settings or at emergency department entry points. These professionals perform the first clinical observations, collect initial information about symptoms, and communicate these findings to physicians who then determine the treatment pathway. In mental-health emergencies in particular, early observations—such as behavioural cues, psychological distress, or risk indicators—can influence diagnostic direction and subsequent psychiatric management. Studies on emergency nursing emphasize that nurses must be trained to identify signs of psychological distress and mental illness in emergency settings because these early assessments can shape treatment decisions and patient safety outcomes.

Because these frontline observations feed directly into clinical decision-making, the training and sensitization of nurses and paramedics is especially important in mental-health care, where symptoms may be subtle, stigmatized, or misinterpreted. Emergency nursing research highlights the need for stronger training in recognizing psychiatric symptoms, communication with distressed patients, and safe triage practices in order to ensure that patients experiencing psychological crises receive appropriate and timely care.

Private Equity Investment in Healthcare

Private equity (PE) firms are investment funds that raise capital from institutional investors such as pension funds, insurance companies, and sovereign wealth funds to acquire companies, improve their financial performance, and later sell them at a profit. These investments typically operate on relatively short time horizons—often three to seven years—and rely on strategies such as operational restructuring, consolidation, and efficiency improvements to increase returns. Economic analyses of private equity investment highlight that these firms prioritize rapid value creation to satisfy investor expectations.

Private equity investment has expanded rapidly in healthcare systems worldwide. A large systematic review published in the British Medical Journal (BMJ) analysing private equity ownership across healthcare providers found that investment activity has increased substantially across hospitals, physician practices, and outpatient facilities. The review reported that private equity ownership was frequently associated with **higher healthcare costs and mixed or negative impacts on quality indicators**, although results varied depending on regulatory environments and healthcare systems.

In addition to cost and quality concerns, private equity investment introduces a structural shift in **decision-making horizons within healthcare institutions**. Unlike traditional hospital promoters or physician-led models, private equity firms typically operate within defined exit timelines, which can influence strategic priorities such as service mix, expansion into high-margin specialties, and optimization of revenue cycles. A systematic review in the British Medical Journal (BMJ) notes that private equity ownership is often associated with operational changes aimed at increasing profitability, including consolidation and cost restructuring, which may not always align with long-term patient care objectives.

Evidence from the United States has raised additional concerns regarding patient outcomes following private equity acquisitions of hospitals. A study published in Journal of the American Medical Association (JAMA) examining Medicare patient data found that hospitals acquired by private equity firms experienced **increases in hospital-acquired complications**, including infections and adverse events, during the years following acquisition. Researchers suggested that operational changes introduced after acquisitions—including staffing adjustments and cost-control strategies—may contribute to these outcomes.

Private equity participation has also grown in emerging healthcare markets such as India. Rising demand for healthcare services, expanding private hospital networks, and increasing insurance coverage have made the sector attractive to global investors. Industry analysis of healthcare investment trends reported that the Indian healthcare sector recorded **over USD 30 billion in mergers, acquisitions, and private equity transactions between 2022 and 2024**, with hospital chains accounting for a significant share of these deals.

While private investment can help expand healthcare infrastructure and improve access to advanced technologies, policy scholars caution that the financial incentives associated with private equity ownership—particularly the pressure to deliver high returns within relatively short investment periods—may conflict with long-term healthcare priorities such as patient safety, workforce stability, and equitable access to care.

International Comparisons: US, UK, and Canada

- **United States:** Empirical studies have linked PE hospital acquisitions with increases in hospital-acquired adverse events and, in some studies, higher mortality in emergency settings; staffing reductions and higher transfer rates have been reported post-acquisition. These findings have triggered policy debates on tighter oversight and disclosure for PE owners.
- **United Kingdom & Canada:** Both nations maintain more dominant public systems (NHS in the UK; predominantly public funding in Canada). Private provision exists but PE penetration has been more limited, and policy levers emphasize public accountability and regulation of private partners. Comparative policy work suggests that public-first systems reduce incentives for short-term profit extraction but raise

other trade-offs (capacity, waiting times).

Costs, Chronic Conditions (Mental Health), and Access Trade-Offs

Private care in India often carries high out-of-pocket costs (consultation fees, bundled diagnostic packages, per-day bed charges). For lifelong, chronic conditions such as schizophrenia, the cumulative financial burden of private care is frequently unsustainable — while public hospitals are cheaper, they are often overburdened and may lack timely access in emergencies. Policy makers must therefore weigh the twin problems of prohibitive private costs and constrained public capacity.

Policy Recommendations

1. **Mandatory clinical representation and qualification on hospital boards** (minimum number/percentage of medically qualified, practicing or recently retired clinicians with voting rights).
2. **Tighter disclosure and limits on PE ownership structures**: mandatory public disclosure of ownership, leverage, and management contracts; scrutiny of staffing and clinical-quality KPIs in transactions.
3. **Strengthen allied/nursing standards**: operationalize National Commission for Allied and Healthcare Professions (NCAHP) regulations and expand certified nursing/paramedical training with mandatory continuing education.
4. **Stricter price transparency and caps on essential and emergency services in India's private healthcare sector**, coupled with targeted public subsidies for long-term mental health care, are essential to mitigate catastrophic out-of-pocket expenditure.

India's private hospitals now sit at the intersection of clinical work and aggressive capital markets. Boardrooms shaped by family holdings, legal and finance professionals, and PE investors risk prioritizing financial metrics over patient-centred outcomes unless governance, regulatory and workforce standards are strengthened. A pragmatic policy mix —

mandatory clinical governance, stricter PE disclosure, investment in allied workforce qualification, and price transparency for essential services — can preserve the benefits of private capital while protecting patient welfare and public interest.

CHAPTER TWENTY-ONE

Pharmacy–Physician Relationship and Drug Prescribing in Private Care

In modern healthcare systems, the relationship between physicians and pharmacies plays a significant role in the delivery of treatment. In hospital settings, particularly in private facilities, patients often obtain medications either through an **in-house hospital pharmacy during admission** or through external retail pharmacies after discharge. While this arrangement improves logistical convenience and ensures immediate drug availability, it can sometimes influence prescribing patterns, particularly where brand-specific medications are recommended instead of generic equivalents.

India's pharmaceutical market is characterized by the presence of **multiple branded versions of the same generic molecule**, often with wide price variations. This creates an environment where prescribing decisions can have a direct impact on patient costs. Studies and policy discussions have noted concerns about the potential influence of pharmaceutical marketing and distribution networks on prescribing behaviour, although these relationships vary widely across institutions and practitioners.

Legal and Regulatory Checks

Several regulatory mechanisms exist in India to mitigate conflicts of interest and protect patients:

1. **Generic Prescription Requirements:** Professional ethics regulations require physicians to prescribe drugs by their **generic names where possible**, encouraging rational drug use and reducing unnecessary costs.
2. **Drug Price Regulation:** The **National Pharmaceutical Pricing Authority (NPPA)** monitors and regulates the prices of many essential medicines under the Drugs (Prices Control) framework to prevent excessive pricing.
3. **Prescription Drug Controls:** The **Drugs and Cosmetics Act and Rules** regulate manufacturing, distribution, and prescription of medicines. For example, drugs listed under **Schedule H** cannot legally be sold without a prescription from a registered medical practitioner.
4. **Generic Drug Access Programs:** Government initiatives such as the **Pradhan Mantri Bharatiya Janaushadhi Pariyojana** promote the availability of quality generic medicines at prices **50–90% lower than branded equivalents**, reinforcing the policy push toward affordability.

Despite regulatory frameworks, isolated cases have surfaced where prescribing patterns appeared to favour specific pharmaceutical brands. For instance, two government doctors under the Central Government Health Scheme were suspended after investigations suggested they were prescribing medicines from a particular pharmaceutical company despite the availability of cheaper alternatives in official supply chains.

Such cases remain exceptions rather than the norm, but they illustrate how prescribing discretion can intersect with market incentives.

Pricing Differences: Hospital vs. External Pharmacies

In many private hospitals, medications supplied through the in-house pharmacy are billed at or near the listed maximum retail price (MRP). By contrast, independent retail pharmacies may offer brand substitutions or generic alternatives at discounted prices, particularly for long-term outpatient prescriptions. Government-supported generic pharmacies demonstrate that the same molecules can be available at substantially lower cost without compromising efficacy.

The physician–pharmacy interface is a necessary component of healthcare delivery, and most clinical decisions are made in the interest of patient care. At the same time, India's regulatory framework—price controls, ethical prescribing norms, and generic medicine programs—exists precisely to reduce the risk that market incentives influence treatment decisions. For patients, awareness of generic alternatives and the option to obtain medicines from outside pharmacies can serve as an additional safeguard within private healthcare settings.

CHAPTER TWENTY-TWO

REFLECTIONS

Given what I have shared so far, I make a humble request to the concerned authorities, both government and medical establishments, to streamline admission processes, especially during emergencies, and more importantly, to prevent the kind of fundamental and human rights violation that occurred in my case.

And somewhere along the way, I feel I may not be alone in this.

I still don't have a resolution. I still don't have a solution.

Based on my understanding and personal experience across two hospitalisations in India and one abroad, I offer the following suggestions:

1. Make the Nominated Representative (NR) Optional

The appointment of an NR should remain a matter of choice, shaped by individual family dynamics. In many cases of schizophrenia, relationships within the family may already be strained, and there may not be a trusted person to take on this responsibility. In such situations, imposing an NR can do more harm than good.

Instead, the focus should shift toward stabilisation through grounding, with attention to sleep, nutrition, and therapeutic support such as CBT. Medication has its place, but overprescription must be approached with caution.

2. Re-evaluate Emergency Sedation Practices

Emergency sedation, as it is often administered, requires urgent re-evaluation. Admissions in such situations can be coercive, raising serious concerns around human and fundamental rights.

In my experience, sedation was initiated even before a psychiatric evaluation, triggering what I can only describe as a memory spiral. This was not temporary disorientation, but a loss of memory that was permanent. Across two hospitalisations in India, I have no recollection of what the first 72 hours of emergency care even looked like, well before any ECTs were introduced exacerbating the permanent memory loss spiral. Even basic experiences such as eating or attending to personal hygiene are absent from memory.

This loss of continuity affects more than just recall. It disrupts the patient's ability to engage meaningfully with treatment. When memory is fragmented, the patient may appear unresponsive or inconsistent, which can then be reflected in clinical assessments such as PANSS scores, without fully accounting for the effects of sedation and memory disruption. In such a state, consent becomes blurred, and control over one's own treatment is difficult to reclaim.

There is also a broader concern that emergency provisions under the MHCA 2017 may be open to misapplication, particularly when sedation precedes evaluation and when authority is exercised without sufficient checks at the point of admission.

A more balanced approach would ensure that a psychiatric evaluation takes place at the earliest possible point of contact, ideally within the patient's personal environment, and that forceful sedation is used only with clear discretion and as a last resort.

3. Strengthen Documentation Around Revocation of Capacity

Capacity is presumed unless clearly documented otherwise. However, in practice, its assessment can become highly subjective. Under the MHCA

2017, capacity is defined by the ability to understand relevant information and the consequences of decisions. A disagreement with the course of treatment, by itself, does not amount to absence of capacity.

In my experience, this line becomes particularly blurred in situations involving induced memory loss. When sedation precedes evaluation and disrupts memory, the patient is left with little ability to recall, respond, or advocate. In such a state, negating capacity becomes easier, while meaningful consent becomes harder to establish.

It is important to note that the episodes themselves did not erase my memory. Prior to emergency sedation, my recall remained intact. The loss of memory followed intervention, not illness. During my third episode abroad, where invasive procedures were suggested but not imposed, I retained full memory of my treatment. My consent was respected. I remember the trajectory of my improvement, my interactions with other patients and caregivers, and the gradual process of stabilisation.

In contrast, during hospitalisations in India, I have no memory of discharge, therapy, or progression, while memories of delusions remained intact. This creates a fragmented recovery, where the patient exits without a coherent understanding of their own treatment journey.

I therefore request the government and State Mental Health Authorities to strengthen oversight, particularly in private establishments. This should include stricter documentation around capacity assessments, regular reassessments, and clear evidence of how and why capacity is overridden, especially in emergency settings.

Periodic review mechanisms, including weekly reassessment of capacity and consent, should be implemented and audited in practice, not just in principle. Additionally, a pattern analysis of emergency admissions, sedation practices, and prolonged revocation of capacity may help identify whether systemic concerns are emerging.

Because I cannot believe this is an isolated experience.

4. Make Advance Directives More Accessible

Based on my experience, there remains a significant gap between the intent of the MHCA 2017 and its implementation. Advance Directives (ADs), though legally recognised, are often met with resistance or inaction. At times, it feels as though there is reluctance to relinquish control, even when the law provides for patient autonomy. I have detailed some of these challenges in Chapter 13.

Capacity exists in a non-hospitalised state, and in many cases, even during hospitalisation. However, in practice, patients with schizophrenia are rarely enabled to make their own treatment decisions. This becomes even more complex in emergency situations, where sedation-induced memory disruption can precede psychiatric evaluation. In such cases, having a pre-drafted AD becomes essential.

Even outside hospital settings, fundamental rights may be compromised in the name of caution. Drafting an AD in one's personal space does not inherently pose a risk to others, and therefore should not be contingent upon extensive psychological assessments. This differs from fitness certifications for work, where risk management may be justified.

Another commonly cited concern is lack of clinical insight. However, under the MHCA 2017, capacity remains the determining factor, not agreement with the treating team. Clinical insight is inherently subjective, and disagreement should not be equated with incapacity.

There is also an inherent contradiction when the same system that questions a patient's insight is responsible for treatment approaches that have disrupted memory and continuity of care.

Finally, procedural barriers such as mandatory notarisation or multiple witnesses make ADs more difficult to execute. Given their deeply personal nature, these requirements should be reconsidered to make the process more accessible and respectful of individual autonomy.

5. Consider a Complete Ban on Electroconvulsive Therapy (ECT)

Electroconvulsive Therapy (ECT), as experienced in my case, raises serious concerns around patient dignity, consent, and long-term cognitive impact. The procedures can feel deeply distressing, and at times, coercive.

In my experience, ECT resulted in permanent memory loss. I have no recollection of the treatment process itself, including any therapeutic interventions such as CBT. At the same time, memories of delusions remained intact. This creates a deeply disorienting imbalance, where the illness is remembered, but the process of healing is not.

This places the patient in a vulnerable position. Questions remain unanswered, the experience of coercion lingers, and the ability to meaningfully participate in care is significantly reduced. In such a state, the patient cannot fully engage in decisions, challenge observations, or reconstruct their own recovery journey, leading to a profound loss of agency.

There are also implications for clinical assessment. Measures such as PANSS scores may not accurately reflect improvement when cognitive factors such as prolonged sedation, high-dose medication, long-acting injectables, and ECT-induced memory loss are involved. When recall itself is impaired, it may appear as though there is little progress or retention, which can then justify further aggressive intervention.

Given these concerns, I believe a complete ban on ECT warrants serious consideration. I have elaborated on this position in detail in Appendix 2.

6. Mandate Patient Satisfaction Surveys

Patient satisfaction surveys should be mandatory across all mental health establishments to capture first-hand patient experience and improve accountability. These must be completed by the patient themselves, not caregivers or Nominated Representatives, to ensure the integrity and authenticity of feedback.

7. Integrate Legal Support at the Point of Admission

Patients should be made aware of their rights at the time of admission, with access to a list of legal professionals who can assist in cases of coercive admission or over-treatment. This safeguard, however, is meaningful only when the patient retains memory of the hospital stay and is able to exercise these rights in real time.

8. Involve Civil Authorities and Independent Support at Admission

The presence of police, civilian authorities, or accredited NGOs at the point of admission can help safeguard patient rights and introduce an element of independent oversight. This can also provide alternative support structures in cases where no Nominated Representative is assigned or where family dynamics are strained.

9. Strengthen Implementation of MHCA 2017 Through Functional MHRBs

The implementation of the MHCA 2017 remains uneven, with Mental Health Review Boards (MHRBs) often inaccessible or non-functional. Strengthening and expanding this network should be prioritised to ensure that existing legal safeguards are meaningfully available to patients.

Rather than focusing solely on expanding public infrastructure, emphasis should also be placed on making current provisions operational. Wherever feasible, MHRB processes such as filing Advance Directives, requesting nomination changes, and submitting complaints should be made accessible through simple and effective online systems.

10. Strengthen Regulation of the Private Medical Sector

In line with the above, if existing infrastructure is to be effectively utilised, stronger regulation of private sector healthcare costs is essential. Rather than announcing new public institutions while current public infrastructure remains strained, the government should prioritise making existing public services functional, and in parallel, encourage a more inclusive and affordable private sector as a practical counterbalance.

Standardised pricing frameworks or caps for critical services can improve affordability and reduce the financial burden on patients. Given that infrastructure expansion and workforce training take time, a regulated and reasonably priced private sector can offer patients greater choice while also easing pressure on public healthcare systems and shortening waiting times.

11. Subsistence Support

With the growing burden of mental health conditions in the country, along with long treatment durations and slow recovery, especially in schizophrenia, it is imperative that subsistence support is strengthened at both the state and central levels to cover rent and basic utilities.

This support should accrue to the patient to encourage independent living and decision-making.

Wherever possible, patients should be encouraged to return to work for better reintegration into society, and employers should be involved with the government in sensitisation and awareness initiatives.

Lastly, while there are some insurance schemes available for persons with disabilities, they largely cover only hospitalisation. Though this is a positive step, more needs to be done to support individuals with lifelong mental health conditions in day-to-day dignified living. This becomes particularly important in schizophrenia, where it is common to be out of work or between jobs due to the slow and extended trajectory of recovery.

Whilst much needs to be done and considered for patients with schizophrenia in India to ensure a dignified life and protect their fundamental and human rights, the enactment of specific acts is in the right spirit.

However, implementation remains uneven. Doctors are given more influence in good faith than may be necessary, and patient consent is often overridden by Nominated Representatives.

I would like to request the government and relevant authorities to make the necessary amendments so that a mental health patient in India continues to feel like a free, consenting adult. At times, the treatment itself leaves deeper psychological gaps due to induced memory loss and related cognitive decline than the ailment itself. And that stays.

I would again like to reiterate the importance of retaining memory and narrative during care:

The erosion of consent, and participation in CBT sessions in a state of memory loss, takes away my grounding. It takes away my lived testimony, to which I have a right. It takes away my ability to participate, and my capacity to filter and internalise what I choose to share in a heightened state and what I choose to hold back. It takes away my autonomy. It takes away my right to consent. And that is where the spiral begins to affect my everyday psychological well-being.

CHAPTER TWENTY-THREE

Holistic Care and Exercise Kit

Remission Care

This chapter is not a prescription, but a gentle toolkit drawn from lived remission.

1. Set Your Circadian Rhythm

This can be supported by gradually reducing dependence on sleep aids or night antipsychotics during remission, wherever medically appropriate. Where possible, a shift toward day-time medication suited to your needs may help.

Night medications can also lead to late-night hunger pangs, which may further disrupt sleep cycles. It helps to minimise or gradually reduce caffeine intake, including coffee and diet sodas. Tapering slowly is important, but shifting to alternatives such as chamomile tea or decaffeinated options can make the transition easier. Additionally, exposing yourself to natural sunlight for about 10 minutes soon after waking, ideally before breakfast, can help regulate your internal clock. Over time, these small adjustments can support a more stable and consistent sleep pattern.

Slowly, but surely.

2. Medication

Please adhere to your medication schedule, including maintenance dosage during remission and beyond, to help prevent relapse. Any changes or tapering should always be done under the guidance of a psychiatrist.

3. Exercise

Start with light exercise, including stretching and gentle walks or slow treadmill sessions. Avoid strength training in the initial six months to one year of remission, as your body may still be recovering from higher medication doses or procedures such as ECT. During this phase, it is important to go easy and allow the body to stabilise.

Gradually, as your strength returns, you can begin to introduce gym-based or strength training routines, starting with a few days a week and increasing at a comfortable pace.

If you experience side effects such as hypnic jerks or tardive dyskinesia, proceed with caution and avoid overexertion. In my experience, intense exercise can aggravate hypnic jerks, so it is best to allow such symptoms to settle before increasing the intensity of your workouts.

4. Talk therapy

If you can find comfort and a level-headed understanding in a relative (rare), then go for it; if not, a friend or a psychologist for talk therapy can certainly help in remission.

In my opinion, the fees need some monitoring in private care, both for psychiatrists and psychologists, since government subsistence is minimal in India for individual patients. At present, the rates are quite high, and the practice is very time-sensitive in my limited experience of six years.

5. Focused Group

Join a dedicated support group for patients, as this can help with reintegration and complement talk therapy. This is something I am still exploring myself.

6. Yoga and Meditation

This can go a long way in helping manage treatment residue. I will suggest some exercises later in this section based on what I have personally tried, though this remains largely exploratory for me. Please consult a trained professional and your psychiatrist before starting yoga or meditation.

7. Affirmation Journal

This can serve as a self-curated form of CBT. You can write down a few affirmations and practise them regularly. Try to read them whenever you are feeling low, or ideally on a daily basis during remission, and even carry them with you during hospitalisation. A sample is provided in Appendix 5.

8. Journaling

Writing is my form of journaling. Identify what works for you and practise it regularly. Once a thought is put into words, the release of that energy can help calm the mind and reduce circular thinking.

If you find yourself running through scenarios in your head, you can write those down as well, perhaps in a simple decision-tree format.

9. Hobby

Pick a hobby, perhaps something from childhood that you enjoyed or aspired to learn and were good at. For me, it is dance, and I plan to explore Indian classical dance, specifically Kathak, starting in 2027.

Slowly, but surely.

10. Substance Abuse

If your psychosis is substance-induced, then please avoid returning to substance use during remission, as this may increase the risk of relapse.

11. Massaging

If culturally appropriate and approved by your medical practitioner, navel oiling and foot massage using a suitable oil may be helpful. I use edible almond oil, but alternatives such as coconut oil can also be used and rotated.

This can help calm the nerves and support the nervous system, and may aid sleep.

Exercise Kit

These practices are intended to support grounding and relaxation, not to induce altered states of consciousness.

For yoga, the following poses may help. You can explore these further online or consult a yoga teacher after receiving approval from your psychiatrist:

1. Cat-Cow Pose
2. Bridge Pose
3. Spine Twist (lying down)
4. Tree Pose

Pranayama practices such as:

- Alternate Nostril Breathing

- Humming Bee
- AUM pronunciation

Avoid Kapalbhati (skull-shining breath), as it may sometimes exacerbate anxiety, especially during remission.

For meditation, please practise under the guidance of a trained practitioner and seek medical clearance beforehand. You can begin with short durations of two to five minutes and gradually increase as you feel comfortable.

You may explore the following approaches:

1. **Focus on your breath**

If focusing on your nostrils feels comfortable, begin there; otherwise, you may focus on the space between your eyebrows. When the mind wanders, gently bring it back. You may set a timer on your phone.

2. **Focus on a mantra**

Choose a mantra you relate to. You may listen to it in the background or silently chant it in your mind while meditating.

3. **Focus on the image of a deity**

You may visualise an image of a deity in your mind or keep one in a familiar place. Look at the image, then close your eyes and recreate it mentally, maintaining your focus on it. You do not need to pray or speak, only to focus.

Avoid candle gazing, as it is not recommended in schizophrenia. If you choose a visual focus, use an image rather than a flame.

Other techniques that one can research and consider practising under the guidance of a practitioner, along with medical clearance, include:

1. **Yoga Nidra**, which can support relaxation and deeper sleep.
2. **Neti-Neti**, meaning "neither this nor that" (the art of negation). If you feel overwhelmed by thoughts, you may gently create distance by reminding yourself: *I am not this body, I am not this thought, I am simply an observer.*

The Way Forward

These are not guarantees, but guardrails drawn from lived experience.

I want to outline the steps a patient, including myself, can take for future episodes. Bygones should be bygones, and it becomes easier when you are not living with your triggers. Going forward, I would try to follow the below, and to a certain extent, I have already made some changes since moving back to India in 2025, as I started to feel better.

1. Voluntary admission.
2. If you are not satisfied with your treatment in India, please consider changing your Nominated Representative. It is your right. NRs play a key role in the Indian treatment framework and should be aligned with the patient. They are meant to support care, not act as proxy decision-makers, as per MHCA 2017.
3. Draft an Advance Directive (a rough template is provided in Appendix 4).
4. Share the Advance Directive with family, friends, your NR, and your consulting psychiatrist
5. Understand the importance of independent living while managing schizophrenia, and try not to become overly dependent.

CHAPTER TWENTY-FOUR

Life After Diagnosis

Life after a diagnosis of schizophrenia is not easy. There is often a constant tussle between choosing to disclose and facing stigma, or keeping it private and accepting the reality as it is. If you choose not to disclose, you may not receive workplace adjustments or support.

Even during remission, it can be difficult to show up every day when motivation is low and the effects of treatment continue to linger. Memory gaps can leave a void, at times making you feel like a culprit rather than the victim.

It is a lived reality.

1. Work Disclosure

Choose, if you can, to discreetly disclose your condition at work and trust the process. If you are in remission, seek and request flexible work arrangements. Be explicit with the in-house psychologist about withdrawal symptoms during remission and the effects of medication on your sleep patterns. This may require certain workplace adjustments.

2. Personal Life

Building a family with such a condition can be challenging. If you plan to get married, decisions around adoption and surrogacy can be complex for mental health patients across the spectrum. Choose a partner who can walk alongside you, at any age and stage.

3. Affirmations

Stay consistent with affirmations and journaling, and practise self-care. Over time, self-care can evolve into self-love and begin to feel more natural. Care for yourself from within. Wherever possible, accept your treatable condition and learn to enjoy your own company. Engage in hobbies you enjoy, and allow yourself to stay relaxed. After all, life is short.

As a parting note, I would like to invite mental health professionals (Indian and international), policymakers, lawyers, and fellow patients to connect with me and engage in conversations on addressing systemic issues such as treatment-induced memory loss and outpatient consent practices.

I would encourage you to reach out for a conversation, or even to connect over a simple cup of coffee.

My LinkedIn URL: www.linkedin.com/in/sakshi-k-author
Please reach out, and I will respond.

Dedication To Fellow Patients

Happiness is...

A dash of hope, but no more dope;
A sigh of relief, but no more grief;
A moment in the present, but no more overthinking;
A self-care routine, but no more messy buns;
A dance of salsa, but no more nachos and cheese;
A cup of chamomile, but no more coffee;
A full-body workout, but no more procrastination;
A full compliance with medication, but no more second-guessing the psychiatrist's opinion;
A voluntary admission and acceptance, but no more tolerance for breaches of consent.

Happiness is self-recovery over self-discovery.
Happiness is a healing me.

Appendix 1: Bridging The Psychological Gap

Author's Note

It all began in November 2019 when I started hearing voices in my head. I was still managing. Very absent-minded and sleep deprived, I started hallucinating by December. I was living alone at that time in India.

It felt different. It felt somewhat unique. It felt liberating. It did not feel sickening.

The energy levels were surprisingly high for a body that was under intermittent catatonia, severely deprived of food, water, and sleep.

The strength of a prolonged acute phase of psychosis was somehow not killing me, even when I remember not sleeping for a long time, now that I look at it in retrospect. I don't remember for how many days I did not sleep. The body was slow but still functioning. But I could be miscalculating and misinterpreting here.

All alone in one of the episodes, I remember fainting on the floor. When I woke up, it felt like a heart attack with no pain. My body trembled, yet I tried to get back up. I still managed to stand after regaining consciousness.

Then again, on a separate occasion, I had no recollection of the last meal I ate. I picked up and ate a discarded piece of chocolate from the dustbin. I don't know why I had discarded it, but I picked it up. And it felt like the feeling of food hitting the stomach lining after a long time.

Subsequently, emergency hospitalization happened. And rightly so.

But how it happened was questionable. The coercion and the barefoot drag are still questionable.

The paramedics entered my personal space at night.

I still feel scared at a knock.

I believe the three coercive emergency admissions were so aggressive and left such a profound impact on me that now I have developed fear.

A phobia of being captured.
Of being hospitalised.

Not because I have been sick.
But because of the misconduct.

I feel I have very limited adult rights living in India now.

I feel intimidated.
I feel overridden.

I don't feel that I live in a democracy anymore.

The treatment on the two occasions of hospitalisation in India led to induced memory spirals at the point of sedative injection, exacerbated by non-consensual ECTs.

The loss of memory I sustained was permanent.

On one occasion, I was made to sign a behaviour agreement restricting my movements, of which I have no memory of signing, and which was part of the discharge summary.

It is my body, then why is the care in India so presumed NR-centric?

In the author's opinion, the work around the emergency and capacity provisions, and the procedural overlap between the two admissions in India, appears systemic and uniform.

It is convenient. An override power that can be exercised without question.

Yet, due to permanent loss of memory and agency, I don't remember any CBT or developing any insight into my ailment.

Till today, the memory of the delusions alone remains intact.

Till today, I question why me?

Is this care?
Or is this responding to reflexive tired bodily agitation with agitation.

They do because they can.

All this has eroded my trust in systems.

I feel oppressed.
I feel depressed.
I feel wronged for being sick.

When you have your lived memories, you connect better, you process better, you respond less aggressively, less instinctively.

You understand better.
You improve faster.
You improve longer.
You prepare for another episode better.

As of March 2026, I requested one of the hospitals, with some basic questions from the discharge summary, to release the paper trail. To release the CBT session notes so that I could assess and analyse what questions were asked and what my responses were, for which I have a permanent memory loss.

After being reduced to a talking toy, the hospital responded after a month, saying that for assisted admissions, they need the written consent of the NR (read presumed NR).

I am not being given the right to recollect my own context, my own words, my own speech,

My own narrative,

Which drove a very transactional and aggressive treatment.

With overlapping treatments — high doses of oral medications, long-acting injections, sedative injections, and repeated anaesthesia-induced ECTs — I spent those twelve long days in what felt like a vegetative state, heavily sedated and cognitively blunted. In that condition, participation, memory, and awareness were almost absent, yet the slowly improving PANSS scores — likely reflecting cognitive blunting rather than recovery — were then used to justify further aggressive procedures.

On the rare occasions when I briefly woke up and tried to understand where I was, the cognitive fog was overwhelming. Before any meaningful awareness could return, the next round of treatment — often another ECT — seemed to erase whatever fragile clarity had begun to emerge.

Where is my agency? Where is the right to my own spoken words? Where is adulting?

This is the psychological gap that remains long after the episode ends.

The Downside of Being Human as a Mental Health Patient

This isolated experience occurred during my treatment abroad at the time of my third episode, where I retained full memory and cognitive awareness. At that point, I was no longer experiencing psychosis, but I was emotionally fragile. The ward environment itself was distressing. Several patients around me were acutely unwell, some aggressive, and one incident involved a physical confrontation. Living in that atmosphere for an extended period left me hypervigilant and unsettled.

Around the same time, I met a friend who came to visit me in the hospital. After returning to my room, the emotional weight of everything I had been holding in surfaced at once. I cried alone. I was grieving the loss of my job, the isolation of being confined in a foreign country, the uncertainty of my future, and the real possibility that my birthday would be spent inside the ward. It was not psychosis. It was grief, exhaustion, and emotional release.

I am an introvert, and during that phase, I did not feel comfortable participating in group therapy sessions. I chose solitude over collective processing, not out of defiance, but out of self-preservation. However, this withdrawal, coupled with emotional expression, was interpreted clinically. Subsequently, a diagnosis of schizoaffective disorder appeared in my discharge summary. This diagnosis was later changed upon request.

What remains unclear to me is what internal clinical trail continues to exist beyond formal correction. More importantly, the experience raised a deeper concern: whether the mental healthcare system leaves space for ordinary human responses to prolonged confinement, fear, and loss, or whether vulnerability itself is too easily absorbed into diagnostic categorisation.

All this, in the name of care, where human emotions sometimes take a back seat.

The Dawn of Acceptance (December 2024 to February 2025)

My first two admissions in India are a blur.

I experienced permanent memory loss following non-consensual invasive procedures for the entire duration of the in-patient stay and a few days after discharge. Because of that, I could not retain or protect my own narrative, the very narrative on which treatment decisions were being based. At times, I felt reduced to a talking toy.

Something changes, however, when you are able to remember your journey.

During treatment abroad, invasive procedures were strongly recommended but not imposed. Rights were protected. Speech was protected. My narrative remained my own.

I remember the trajectory of my recovery.
I remember being rude. I remember becoming calmer.
Most importantly, I remember the people I met.

Meeting other individuals on the same spectrum changed my perspective. Through those conversations, I slowly came to accept something difficult but necessary:

I have a mental health problem.

Later, as I improved and prepared for discharge, I saw newly admitted patients in their vulnerability. Their symptoms overlapped with my own past behaviour.

And again, the realization became clear:

I have a mental health problem.

This is why consent and the retention of memory are so important in long-term recovery.

Unfortunately, this is a point that is still often lost within the Indian mental healthcare system.

Appendix 2: An Appeal To The Hon'ble Supreme Court Of India

Date: March 8, 2026

May the Imminent Change be seen Clearly before it is too Late.

May Mental Peace Abide.

Subject: Appeal for Call to Action

1. Please Ban ECT and Emergency Sedation in India

Coercive sedation, even before examination by a psychiatrist, by invading the personal space of a patient, leaves long-lasting psychological gaps as the last lived memory before the onset of the spiral. Exacerbated by ECTs, the spiral strengthens, and the memory loss of the hospital stay is permanent. It leaves the memory of the delusions intact. However, therapy gets washed away. And the same insight that this therapy builds is then subsequently questioned when the patient wants to exercise fundamental rights under the Indian Constitution to draft a document of her care in her personal space. The same insight that the same medical establishments wash away because of invasive, non-consensual procedures.

When memory is impaired, you don't just lose self-control and your testimony, your reflexes become defensive, your brain beckons for a recall under heavy sedation. The brain wants to accept and understand. The brain wants to stop the instinctive words flowing out and understand the context and be more structured.

The brain is tortured further instead when PANSS sessions don't stick due to permanent memory loss. It all becomes circular, to no long-term gain.

The handful of flashes are alive. The food isn't. The hygiene isn't. The flashes for the fight for restoration of consent which was brazenly taken away both times in India.

As if they know exactly what to do in a field that's more observational than diagnostic.

How fair is this? The victim gets victimised. The marginal gets marginalised. The sick feels sicker and more violated and even more aggressive. Relationships spoil. Loneliness survives. Understanding blunts. Loneliness survives.

The sick gets reduced to a talking prop. Having no recollection of her own speech. Her own words. Her own testimony deciding her fate.

Are criminals denied their right to a lived and memory-driven testimony that decides their fate?

Are we treating mental health patients worse than criminals in this country?
By dragging them barefoot and by breaking into their personal space?

Is this all convenient, rehearsed, and structural?
Is this systemic?

Are we making criminals of mental health patients in India?

Are we creating oppression and dissent so profound?

That the innocent and naïve mind loses control.
Just because it does not want to relinquish control and decision-making powers to the presumed NR?
Is capacity so hard to retrieve and retain if it had not been for the induced spiral?

A mental health patient wants to feel adult in India.

A consenting adult.

2. Fundamental Rights of Patients with Mental Health Disability in the Remission and Non-hospitalised state

My attempt to draft and file my own Advance Directive since Oct 2025 has failed. Instead, in a stable state and in a non-hospitalised state, I have not been able to draft a document of my own care, when even in a hospitalised state I am presumed to have the capacity to decide the course of my treatment.

I have capacity when I can understand the relevant information and consequences. I don't need to agree with the medical treatment for the course of treatment. I should be allowed to make a choice. I should be allowed to disagree.

However, my clinical insight is questioned by an open-ended prescription after a breach of patient-doctor confidentiality, when I was asked to share the draft of my AD over WhatsApp with customer support multiple times in Oct 2025.

Further, my request to retrieve my own file, my own testimony and words as an adult, to understand my overly aggressive treatment better, is being denied in the name of assisted admission. I am again asked to get written consent from my presumed NR in a stable, non-hospitalised state. It's very worrisome.

I have lived independently since 18 years of age. My adult rights are not being respected. I am being made to run from pillar to post to exercise fundamental rights under the Indian Constitution as a mental health patient, after my human rights have been repeatedly violated.

I strongly suggest that, in the light of growing mental health issues in India amongst independent living and consenting adults of my age and younger (millennials and Gen Z), the clause of having a nominated representative be made optional.

Capacity should exist, and it does exist, even in an episode, but for the induced spiral.

Focus should be on sleep stabilisation, food, and water.

3. MHCA Implementation

I would request the Supreme Court of India to ask the Government to take concrete steps to implement the MHCA 2017 by establishing MHRBs at the state and district levels.

MHRBs are virtually non-existent as of March 2026, even after nine years of the Act's enactment. The implementation continues to be patchy, and patients have very limited means for redressal.

4. Strict Regulations Around Private Care

I would request the Supreme Court of India to ask the Government of India for strict regulations around private care fees. The private care charges for mental healthcare are exorbitant, and the residential packages are promoted more like holiday packages than treatment packages. Even remission costs are very expensive per session with the psychiatrist.

If I were looking for a holiday, I would definitely prefer wilderness and not their overpriced packages.

Further, strict regulation of private sector healthcare would also lead to better management of public healthcare with limited and constrained resources. Patients will have more affordable choice, and we can make better use of the existing infrastructure with immediate effect, instead of piling on public health infrastructure announcements in budgets when the ground reality for implementation of MHCA and related MHRBs is still lagging. These over-ambitious announcements just put extra pressure on the existing infrastructure. Further, this pushes the matter of patient rights and redressal even further away.

Though I understand that medical tourism is good for the country's economy, I stand opposed to the promotion of residential care packages as PR packages at premium rates. This makes care affordable only to the elite section of society.

Care has to remain basic, humane, and non-incentivised, which isn't the case in private sector care in India, now heavily driven by private equity firms.

I would like to reiterate my stance that permanent memory loss in mental healthcare is a serious concern for long-term patient well-being. It washes away therapy. The memory of coercive admission, forced sedation, and delusions remains intact.

This is a very dangerous proposition, and this must stop, please.

Appendix 3: Emotional Scarring—a Note To Self

Date: March 15, 2026

Just the backlog of fragmented personal relationships.

The cognitive load of three episodes.

The impaired memories of medical treatment.

The lived memories of my delusions and my mistreatment.

It's all a bit too much.

A bit too much to endure.
A bit too much to push through.

What's holding me together is the acceptance of my lived reality, while the lost memories of my own narratives during my two treatments in India beckon.

A beckoning so strong, yet so unheard that I fail to feel like an independent adult.

As if my fundamental and human rights are not the same as yours.

Appendix 4: Advance Directive For Mental Health Care

Name:
Date of Birth:
Address:
Contact Number:

Date of Drafting:

1. Declaration

I, the undersigned, am making this Advance Directive in a stable state of mind. I am able to understand the nature and consequences of this document.

This document reflects my preferences for mental health treatment in the event that I am unable to make decisions during a future episode.

2. Treatment Preferences

- I prefer treatment that is **least invasive.**
- I prefer a focus on **sleep stabilisation, food, hydration, and a calm environment.**
- I prefer to be treated with **respect, dignity, and clear communication** at all times.

3. Treatments I Do Not Consent To

- I do **not consent to Electroconvulsive Therapy (ECT).**
- I do **not consent to forced or coercive sedation without prior evaluation by a psychiatrist,** except in immediate life-threatening situations.
- I do **not consent to any invasive procedure without my informed**

consent wherever possible.

4. Consent and Capacity

- I wish to be treated as a **consenting adult** wherever I demonstrate the ability to understand and communicate.
- I reserve the **right to ask questions, disagree, and make choices** regarding my treatment.

5. Access to Records

- I request full access to my **medical records, therapy notes, and treatment history** upon request.
- My records should not be withheld from me when I am in a stable and non-hospitalised state.

6. Nominated Representative (Optional)

Name (if any):
Relationship:
Contact:

I understand that I may appoint a Nominated Representative. However, I prefer that my **own consent and decision-making be prioritised** wherever I have capacity.

7. Review and Revocation

I understand that I can **review, modify, or revoke** this Advance Directive at any time when I am in a stable state of mind.

Signature:
Name:
Date:

Witness 1 (Name & Signature):
Witness 2 (Name & Signature):

This document reflects my personal preferences and my right to dignity, autonomy, and informed consent in mental healthcare.

Appendix 5: Affirmations

Author's Note

These affirmations were written from a place of calm and recovery. They gather what I've learned—through hospitalization, through release, and through the quiet understanding that comes after both. They aren't confessions; they're reminders. If you're reading this during an episode, or after one, may these words help you hold on to yourself a little longer. Healing begins when you start talking to your own mind with kindness.

1. No one wants to harm me. I am the best version of myself. The noises in my head aren't true. They are just a reflection of stress and my current thought process.
2. I need to adhere to my medication regimen to quieten my head.
3. I do not need non-consensual invasive treatments. I need healthy food, lots of water, and aided sleep.
4. I do not need overdosing of anti-psychotics. I need other optional sleep aids for a night's rest.
5. I want to remember. I wish to observe.
6. I don't need a lot of people around me every day. I need to be left alone to process my feelings.
7. I need a bar of chocolate every day.
8. I need to cut back or stop caffeine.
9. I need to take care of my physical health, including my hygiene.
10. I need light yoga, long walks, lots of laughter, and basic meditation.
11. I need one cheat meal a week, and I need to keep a check on my weight.
12. I need a morning medication instead of a night medication as my maintenance dose, one that is light on my system so that I don't get hunger pangs. If I do get pangs, they can be managed during the day, balanced with moderate exercise. No more night binging.
13. I have the right to my fertility under all circumstances. I have the right to have the option of starting a family. Please prescribe a medicine suitable to my age, gender, and fertility as a maintenance dose.
14. When I cry, it does not mean it's psychosis. When I get angry, it does not

mean it's psychosis. Please stop over-analysing and labelling every move as psychosis. Please treat me as a human, and be humane.

15. To the rebukes, in family or otherwise: Please get a life and go to hell. Prima facie, you will only meet my silence. But this line is for you in print.
16. To my well-wishers: Thank you, even with limited understanding.
17. You can recover fully. If not, you can manage your symptoms through affirmative talk. Self-talk or journaling should be encouraged, even during an episode. Even if the ideas are delusional, the process of writing gives the brain a reset. Once you write something down, you automatically think about it less. This should not attract an extra dose of an anti-psychotic, but compassion. Please give the patient time to pivot to centre. Encourage journaling without too much judgment.
18. I want to be independent and live my own life. I want to have a work and family life. Living alone gives me freedom of choice. I want to focus back.
19. I want to feel the sunlight again on my skin. I want to breathe natural air again. I wish to integrate back.
20. I want to come out, in my own way, with my ailment: to my family, to my friends, and to my employers. I wish myself luck.

References

Chapter 1

1. World Health Organization. (2025, October 6). *Schizophrenia* [Fact sheet]. World Health Organization. https://www.who.int/news-room/fact-sheets/detail/schizophrenia
2. WebMD. (2024, March 11). *Schizophrenia symptoms.* https://www.webmd.com/schizophrenia/schizophrenia-symptoms
3. Verywell Mind. (2024, January 23). *The relationship between schizophrenia and dopamine.* Verywell Mind. https://www.verywellmind.com/the-relationship-between-schizophrenia-and-dopamine-5219904
4. NHS. (2025). Schizophrenia causes. NHS. https://www.nhs.uk/mental-health/conditions/schizophrenia/causes/

Chapter 6

1. NAMI. (2024, August). *Long-acting injectables (LAIs).* https://www.nami.org/treatments-and-approaches/mental-health-medications/long-acting-injectables-lais/
2. National Institute of Mental Health. (2024, February). *Psychotherapies.* https://www.nimh.nih.gov/health/topics/psychotherapies
3. Cleveland Clinic. (2025, May 26). *Electroconvulsive therapy (ECT).* https://my.clevelandclinic.org/health/treatments/9302-ect-electroconvulsive-therapy
4. Mayo Clinic. (2023, April). *Transcranial magnetic stimulation.* https://www.mayoclinic.org/tests-procedures/transcranial-magnetic-stimulation/about/pac-20384625
5. Yi, S., Wang, Q., Wang, W., Hong, C., & Ren, Z. (2024). *Efficacy of repetitive transcranial magnetic stimulation (rTMS) on negative symptoms and cognitive functioning in schizophrenia: An umbrella review of systematic*

reviews and meta-analyses. Psychiatry Research, 333, 115728. https://doi.org/10.1016/j.psychres.2024.115728

Chapter 10

1. Dilsaver, S. C. (1992). *Differentiating organic from functional psychosis. American Family Physician, 45*(3), 1173–1180.https://pubmed.ncbi.nlm.nih.gov/1543102/
2. Nicotra, E., Casu, G., Piras, S., & Marchese, G. (2015). *On the use of the Positive and Negative Syndrome Scale in randomized clinical trials. Schizophrenia Research, 165*(2–3), 181–187. https://doi.org/10.1016/j.schres.2015.04.006
3. Rahman, S. M., Abduelmula, A., & Jafferany, M. (2023). *Psychopathological symptoms in dermatology: A basic approach toward psychocutaneous disorders. International Journal of Dermatology, 62*(3), 346–356.https://doi.org/10.1111/ijd.16344

Chapter 14

1. Jutla, A., Foss-Feig, J., & Veenstra-VanderWeele, J. (2021). *Autism spectrum disorder and schizophrenia: An updated conceptual review. Autism Research, 15*(3), 384–412. https://doi.org/10.1002/aur.2659
2. Cherney, K. (2026, January 30). *Autism vs. schizophrenia: Is there a link?* Healthline. https://www.healthline.com/health/autism-vs-schizophrenia
3. Autism Speaks. (2025). *Levels of autism.* Autism Speaks. https://www.autismspeaks.org/levels-of-autism
4. Healthline. (2025, March 13). *Bipolar disorder vs. schizophrenia: What's the difference?* https://www.healthline.com/health/bipolar-disorder/bipolar-vs-schizophrenia
5. World Health Organization. (2025, August 29). *Depressive disorder (depression).* World Health Organization. https://www.who.int/news-room/fact-sheets/detail/depression

Chapter 15

1. Hor, K., & Taylor, M. (2010). *Suicide and schizophrenia: A systematic review of rates and risk factors.* Journal of Psychopharmacology, 24(4_suppl), 81–90. https://pmc.ncbi.nlm.nih.gov/articles/PMC2951591/

Chapter 16

1. Rao, R. (2019). *Mental Healthcare Act, 2017, and addiction treatment.* Indian Journal of Psychological Medicine, 41(2), 109–113. https://pmc.ncbi.nlm.nih.gov/articles/PMC6425793/
2. Government of Karnataka. (2020). *e-MANAS: Karnataka Mental Healthcare Management System.* Department of Health and Family Welfare. https://e-manas.karnataka.gov.in/
3. Rakshit, D. (2021, April 12). *Delhi HC orders probe into mental health care review board, patient complaint process.* The Swaddle. https://www.theswaddle.com/delhi-hc-orders-probe-into-mental-health-care-review-board-patient-complaint-process
4. Math, S. B., Gowda, G. S., Basavaraju, V., Manjunatha, N., Kumar, C. N., Enara, A., & Thirthalli, J. (2019). *Cost estimation for the implementation of the Mental Healthcare Act 2017.* Indian Journal of Psychiatry, 61(Suppl 4), S650–S659. https://journals.lww.com/indianjpsychiatry/fulltext/2019/61004/cost_estimation_for_the_implementation_of_the.8.aspx
5. Government of India. (2017). *The Mental Healthcare Act, 2017 (Act No. 10 of 2017).* Ministry of Law and Justice. https://www.indiacode.nic.in/bitstream/123456789/2249/1/A2017-10.pdf

Chapter 17

1. Goswami, S. (2026, February 1). *Union Budget 2026: New national-level mental health institutes to be set up.* NDTV. https://www.ndtv.com/

health/union-budget-2026-national-level-mental-health-institutes-to-be-set-up-10923638

2. Atypical Advantage. (2024, February 2). *List of government schemes for disabled persons in India: Empowerment and inclusion guide.* https://atypicaladvantage.in/atypical-blog/post/list-of-government-schemes-for-disabled-persons-in-india-empowerment-and-inclusion-guide

Chapter 18

1. Balakrishnan, A., Kulkarni, K., Moirangthem, S., Kumar, C. N., Math, S. B., & Murthy, P. (2019). *The Rights of Persons with Disabilities Act 2016: Mental health implications.* Indian Journal of Psychological Medicine, 41(2), 119–125. https://www.ncbi.nlm.nih.gov/pmc/articles/PMC6436405/
2. Johari, B. (2024, June 24). *India's rights of persons with disabilities act 2016: An unfulfilled promise.* Oxford Human Rights Hub. https://ohrh.law.ox.ac.uk/indias-rights-of-persons-with-disabilities-act-2016-an-unfulfilled-promise/
3. Sharda, S. (2023, October 10). *The 'invisible' disability of mental illness: Barriers to social security access.* Ideas for India. https://www.ideasforindia.in/topics/human-development/the-invisible-disability-of-mental-illness-challenges-of-social-security-access
4. Times News Network. (2025, March 5). *Over 3k hearing-impaired persons struggle for disability certificates.* The Times of India. https://timesofindia.indiatimes.com/city/bareilly/over-3k-hearing-impaired-persons-struggle-for-disability-certificates/articleshow/118741482.cms
5. U.S. Department of Justice. (2020). *A guide to disability rights laws.* ADA.gov. https://www.ada.gov/resources/disability-rights-guide/
6. Lichfields. (n.d.). *Health and wellbeing policy.* https://lichfields.uk/health-and-wellbeing/policy
7. Times News Network. (2024, August 7). *For less than 40% disability, govt plans white UDID card.* The Times of India. https://timesofindia.indiatimes.com/city/pune/for-less-

than-40-disability-govt-plans-white-udid-card/articleshow/11233269cms

8. Prakash, O. (2024). *Redefining disability certification for mental illness in India: Towards global standards and functional assessments. Indian Journal of Psychiatry,* 66(9), 863–867. https://doi.org/10.4103/indianjpsychiatry.indianjpsychiatry_435_24
9. Bachhav, A. K., Sharma, H. B., & Singhai, K. M. (2025). *Challenges in disability certification in psychiatry in India. Indian Journal of Psychiatry,* 67(7), 707–709.https://doi.org/10.4103/indianjpsychiatry_959_24
10. MU, S. (2020, April 14). *Guide to government schemes for the mentally disabled.* Cadabam's Hospitals. https://www.cadabamshospitals.com/guide-to-government-schemes-for-the-mentally-disabled/

Chapter 19

1. Digital Personal Data Protection Act, 2023. (2023). https://www.dpdpact2023.com/
2. KPMG in India. (2025, December 19). *The privacy prescription: Impact of DPDP Act and rules in healthcare and life sciences sector.* https://kpmg.com/in/en/insights/2025/12/the-privacy-prescription-impact-of-dpdp-act-and-rules-in-healthcare-and-life-sciences-sector.html
3. KPMG in India. (2025, December). *The privacy prescription: Impact of DPDP Act and rules in healthcare and life sciences sector.* https://assets.kpmg.com/content/dam/kpmgsites/in/pdf/2025/12/the-privacy-prescription-impact-of-dpdp-act-and-rules-in-healthcare-and-life-sciences-sector.pdf.coredownload.pdf
4. KALP Systems. (2026, February 14). *Healthcare data security challenges under the India DPDP Act.* https://kalpsystems.com/dpdp/healthcare-data-security-dpdp-india/
5. Meridian Bridge Strategy. (2026, February 27). *DPDP compliance costs for Indian healthcare: Safeguarding patient data & your bottom line.* https://www.dpdpworkshop.com/learn/dpdp-cost-healthcare

Chapter 20

1. Hunter, B. M., Murray, S. F., Marathe, S., & Chakravarthi, I. (2022). *Decentred regulation: The case of private healthcare in India. World Development, 155,* 105889. https://doi.org/10.1016/j.worlddev.2022.105889
2. Grant Thornton Bharat. (n.d.). *Vitals for growth: Decoding healthcare financing and funding in India.* https://www.grantthornton.in/insights/thought-leadership/vitals-for-growth-decoding-healthcare-financing-and-funding-in-india/
3. Farooqui, A., John, S., & Raychaudhari, P. S. (2025). Corporate governance and financial performance in Indian private healthcare: A literature review and conceptual framework. South Eastern European Journal of Public Health. https://www.researchgate.net/publication/390475269
4. Bhat, R., & Jain, N. (2006, March). *Governance of private sector corporate hospitals and their financial performance: Preliminary observations based on listed and unlisted hospitals in India* (Working Paper No. 2006-03-08). Indian Institute of Management Ahmedabad. https://www.iima.ac.in/sites/default/files/rnpfiles/2006-03-07rbhat.pdf
5. Dibbs, R., Ferry, A., Reece, E., & Buchanan, E. P. (2021). *Composition of governing boards within top-grossing hospitals: A cross-sectional study. Plastic and Reconstructive Surgery Global Open,* 9(10S), 161–162. https://doi.org/10.1097/01.GOX.0000799940.71433.a4
6. The Diligent team. (2018, September 18). *What is the composition of a hospital board of directors?* Diligent. https://www.diligent.com/resources/blog/what-is-the-composition-of-a-hospital-board-of-directors
7. Basu, S., Andrews, J., Kishore, S., Panjabi, R., & Stuckler, D. (2012). *Comparative performance of private and public healthcare systems in low- and middle-income countries: A systematic review. PLOS Medicine, 9*(6), e1001244. https://doi.org/10.1371/journal.pmed.1001244
8. World Health Organization. (2021, August 3). *Global patient safety action plan 2021–2030.* https://www.who.int/publications/i/item/9789240032705
9. Peta, D., Day, A., Lugari, W. S., Gorman, V., Ahayalimudin, N., & Pajo, V. M. T. (2023). *Triage: A global perspective. Journal of Emergency Nursing,*

49(6), 814–825. https://doi.org/10.1016/j.jen.2023.08.004

10. de Lacy, J. (2011). Improving the assessment and triage of patients with mental illness attending the emergency department (Master's dissertation, Royal College of Surgeons in Ireland). https://repository.rcsi.com/articles/thesis/10811375
11. Chou, H.-J., & Tseng, K.-Y. (2020). *The experience of emergency nurses caring for patients with mental illness: A qualitative study. International Journal of Environmental Research and Public Health, 17*(22), 8540. https://doi.org/10.3390/ijerph17228540
12. Dizavandi, F. R., Froutan, R., Karimi Moonaghi, H., Ebadi, A., & Fayyazi Bordbar, M. R. (2023). *Mental health triage from the viewpoint of psychiatric emergency department nurses: A qualitative study. Archives of Academic Emergency Medicine, 11*(1), e70. https://pmc.ncbi.nlm.nih.gov/articles/PMC10646953
13. Alharthi, A. A., Alammari, M. S. M., & Alrashidi, A. F. (2024). *The role of paramedics and nurses in managing mental health crises in pre-hospital settings. International Journal of Scientific and Research Publications, 14*(11), 187–195. https://www.ijsrp.org/research-paper-1124/ijsrp-p15525.pdf
14. AlShibi, A. N., & Hamdan-Mansour, A. M. (2020, April 16). *Nurses' knowledge and skills to manage patients with psychological distress in emergency departments. The Open Nursing Journal, 14*, 49. https://www.opennursingjournal.com/VOLUME/14/PAGE/49/FULLTEXT/
15. Investopedia. (n.d.). *Private equity.* https://www.investopedia.com/terms/p/privateequity.asp
16. Borsa, A., Bejarano, G., Ellen, M., & Bruch, J. D. (2023). *Evaluating trends in private equity ownership and impacts on health outcomes, costs, and quality: Systematic review. BMJ, 382*, e075244. https://www.bmj.com/content/382/bmj-2023-075244
17. Kannan, S., Bruch, J. D., & Song, Z. (2023). *Changes in hospital adverse events and patient outcomes associated with private equity acquisition. JAMA, 330*(24), 2365–2375. https://jamanetwork.com/journals/jama/fullarticle/2813379
18. Miller, J. (2023, December 26). *What happens when private equity takes over a hospital.* Harvard Medical School. https://hms.harvard.edu/news/what-happens-when-private-equity-takes-over-hospital
19. The Guardian. (2025, October 14). *Private equity takeover of hospitals led*

to rise in Medicare emergency patient deaths, says study. https://www.theguardian.com/us-news/2025/oct/14/private-equity-hospitals-medicare-patient-deaths

20. Remedies Project. (n.d.). *What countries have free healthcare and better outcomes?* https://remediesproject.com/what-countries-have-free-healthcare-and-better-outcomes
21. BioSpectrum India. (2025, March 11). *India's healthcare and pharma sector records deals over $30 billion from 2022 to 2024.* https://www.biospectrumindia.com/news/101/25821/indias-healthcare-and-pharma-sector-records-deals-over-30-b-from-2022-to-2024.html
22. Chinchu, C. (2023). *Balancing regulation and autonomy: NCAHP Act and the psychology profession in India. Indian Journal of Psychological Medicine.* https://pmc.ncbi.nlm.nih.gov/articles/PMC11268281/

Chapter 21

1. Agarwal, A. (2025, April 22). *Do doctors get commission for prescribing drugs – Doctor Commission*. Medkart Pharmacy. https://www.medkart.in/blog/understanding-the-commission-nexus-between-doctors-hospitals-and-mrs-in-india
2. Neelakantan, M. (2022, August 27). *The doctor-drug company nexus: Diagnosis and treatment*. SCC Online Blog. https://www.scconline.com/blog/post/2022/08/27/the-doctor-drug-company-nexus-diagnosis-and-treatment/
3. Biplab, L., Jain, K., & Rajkumar, P. (2023, July 31). *Encapsulating the branded vs. generics debate: Pitfalls and doctors' dilemma*. India Corporate Law. https://corporate.cyrilamarchandblogs.com/2023/07/encapsulating-the-branded-vs-generics-debate-pitfalls-and-doctors-dilemma/
4. National Pharmaceutical Pricing Authority. (n.d.). *National Pharmaceutical Pricing Authority*. Wikipedia. Retrieved March 26, 2026, from https://en.wikipedia.org/wiki/National_Pharmaceutical_Pricing_Authority
5. Drugs and Cosmetics Rules, 194 (n.d.). *Drugs and Cosmetics Rules, 1945.*

Wikipedia.
Retrieved March 26, 2026, from https://en.wikipedia.org/wiki/Drugs_and_Cosmetics_Rules%2C_1945

6. Schedule H. (n.d.). *Schedule H.* Wikipedia. Retrieved March 26, 2026, from https://en.wikipedia.org/wiki/Schedule_H
7. Pradhan Mantri Bharatiya Janaushadhi Pariyojana. (n.d.). *Pradhan Mantri Bharatiya Janaushadhi Pariyojana.* Wikipedia. Retrieved March 26, 2026, from https://en.wikipedia.org/wiki/Pradhan_Mantri_Bharatiya_Janaushadhi_Pariyojana
8. Barsha Misra. (2022, July 4). *Breaking pharma doctor nexus: Union health minister suspends 2 CGHS doctors for favouring one pharma company drugs.* Medical Dialogues. https://medicaldialogues.in/news/health/doctors/breaking-pharma-doctor-nexus-union-health-minister-suspends-2-cghs-doctors-for-favouring-one-pharma-company-drugs-95443

About The Author

Sakshi.k is an auditor by profession with over eleven years of experience working across India, the UK, and Canada. She holds an MBA, is a CPA (US), has cleared two levels of the US CFA program, and graduated with a B. Com (Honours) from Lady Shri Ram College.

An avid reader with a keen interest in current affairs, her inclination toward reflective writing emerged in 2025 following personal circumstances that led her to turn inward and temporarily engage less with the external world. Her writing reflects this period of introspection and quiet observation.

Other Book By The Author

- Shades I: Thoughts that Linger...

www.ingramcontent.com/pod-product-compliance
Lightning Source LLC
LaVergne TN
LVHW100316210926
848480LV00003B/1146